? ילדתך לשון ך
פרה פרה
אברהם גיל

ZEH KAPOROSI זה כפרתי

AVROHOM REIT

ZEH זה כפרתי

KAPOROSI

CUSTOM OF KAPOROS

ZEH KAPAROSI

Mosaica Press, Inc.
© 2013 by Mosaica Press

Edited by Doron Kornbluth
Designed by Chana Wagner
Typeset by Daniella Kirsch

ISBN 978-1-937-88705-6   ISBN-10: 1-937-88705-7

To contact the author: 347.407.1239

Published and distributed by:

Mosaica Press, Inc.
www.mosaicapress.com
info@mosaicapress.com
Printed in Israel

CONTENTS

Rabbi Y. Belsky
506 EAST 7th STREET
BROOKLYN, NEW YORK 11218

ישראל הלוי בעלסקי
941 - 0112

הנה הרב ר' יוברתם ריין נ"י הרצוד ל' ברי או וכצל
הנוכחי "כבר נגל ז' ענין מנהג כמרת שמסבבים
לפני יום הכיפורים בתרנגולים, ופתב ג'אור מקום אם לל
התמסאם, וצלאת צלא מ' שלבו מברא חכמת ותהלון לבל
שורש כל גבל יצרו הנגצ צ'ם ינקזו צ' סיבוחן כמבקי
ערב ר' יוברתם ל' ותמצא זו ג'אור התוצו מהתצ'ע
ג'אור נבון כל פנ' ובג'ב ירוה מוון צאש
לבנ' יהודא קלת הבצו כתוצה ט' סבר פצוך
עצקד יום כ"ב פתן יס"ו צ' צל צ' פצך
ישראל הלוי בעלסקי

מתיבתא תפארת ירושלים
MESIVTHA TIFERETH JERUSALEM
145 EAST BROADWAY / NEW YORK, NY 10002

RABBI DOVID FEINSTEIN
ROSH HAYESHIVA

RABBI CHAYIM GANZWEIG
MASHGIACH

<u>מכתב ברכה</u>

יום בשורה הוא לנו שידידי הרב היקר ר' אברהם יצחק
ר"ח שליט"א שהוא מחשובי חברי הכולל בית מדרש
לתורה והוראה ע"י הישיבה הקדושה מתיבתא
תפארת ירושלים אשר ג' שהוא עומד להוציא לאור
זולת ספרו החשוב בענין ד' מינים.

כבתו היי כתלי דבי מדרשא הלל"ת כי כ' שהי' לו אולם
עם מורינו ורבינו ראש הישיבה שליט"א בבה"מ ועינינו
הלכה וכן בעינינו הי' ד'זוכים בענין הוראה.

ולכן אני שמח כא לחוות דעתי בענין חובן הספר הל'
מ"א בהבור לאחד ירה כאתי לאור שהתחבר כחבר יחב
אכא יולו' דבר מתוק יזווכו' ואנוש' כרף לבלא יכא יותר
ויהון לסעות לציבור הרחב לקיים מצות ד' מינים כתיקונה
ונצבה ש"י זה יתיחד כל יקולו לצוגות הדורן ית',
והדר האחבר הלב ילל'ת דכא דכא אשר יפנה להפיל
אדי עותיו חולה ורביים יהנו אמנו
כ'רכירת חיים יאיל בלבלוויץ
ל'ב ללול הפ"ל

הנ' ידידי שליט"א הלב שסגן הלב הולזא לאור ניב ספרים כאלזל הסה"ב"
ותקבלו ברבון אלל הביבר הרחב והוא צד"ן אכאל ש"ר בית אזרוינו
ואק"ח הקר זא אמר רל' שליט"א ונראת אול ספר זא פ' זוכו דעון
בבריות ו"ר שיתחן כניל דכא ואר יפנה ילל'ת
כ'רכירת חיים יאיקא בלבלוויץ - ט"ז אדר הק"ל

בית המדרש עמק הלכה
BETH MEDRASH EMEK HALACHA

בית מדרשו של רבנו הגאון רב טובי' גולדשטיין זצוק"ל

הרב משה אשר ראטענד
ראש הישיבה

יום ג' לס' שופטים א' אלול תשנ"ה

הנה ידי"נ הרה"ג ר' אברהם חיים שליט"א הביא לפני קונטרס
אסא מרא הענין כמנהג וסיבו מאת אשכול ופענוח של
העמשא, וכמה דברים שם ציון רב אמרנא נאה ולמעלה. וכן
קונטרס ... אשר הביא לדין ... גילה ... ...
והביא אלא הרבה טוב מאד ... לבזו ... אם הבאתי ...
13 ...
... ...

ואאחל הכא לכבוד ... ...
מלמעלה. וישאו ... ברכה, ... לטובה.

חתים לכה ... ...
ידי"נ ... ...

משה אשר ראטנד

P O Box 300-006 • 1288 Coney Island Avenue • Brooklyn, NY 11230 • Phone 718-232-1600 • Fax 718-701-5686

בס"ד, ירושלים עיה"ק ת"ו, מוצאי חג הפסח תשע"ג

לכבוד מעלת מזכה הרבים
הרה"ג **אברהם רייט** שליט"א

בשמחה ובהנאה מרובה קראתי את כתב היד של ספרך החשוב והשימושי '**כפר נא**', המבאר בבהירות ובפרוטרוט, את כל ענייני מנהג הכפרות שנהגו בו ישראל קדושים. בלשון אנגלית בהירה נהירה ומהירה, הנך מוביל את הקורא בכל שלבי קיום המנהג, החל מיסודות מקורותיו עד ההנהגה הלכה למעשה בזמן הזה.
המייחד את הספר הוא כדרכך בקודש בסדרת '**תקופת השנה**', לשתף את הקוראים הלא מנוסים - בעצות מעשיות מניסיונך העשיר להקל על הפרטים הטכניים של פעולות המצוה, ומתקנינו בעצה טובה מסולאה בפז שלא נוכל למצוא בספרים או בשיעורים.
ראוי ספר זה להדריך את הניגשים לערוך כפרות, למען ידעו את הדרך ילכו בה ואת המעשה אשר יעשון.

בברכת התורה והמצווה
אמתי בן-דוד

נ.ב. קונטרס 'כפר נא' הוא כל כך מפורט ויפה עד שאין לי כמעט מה להעיר עליו. קראתי בעיקר מפרק חמישי עד פרק יג, בדברים הנוגעים לענייני שחיטה ומצוותיה.
מכל מקום אציין דבר אחד, **פרק י.** יש טעם נוסף לכיסוי הדם בחיות, בספר ארחות חיים (בסוף 'דין כסוי הדם') והכלבו (סוף סי' קח).

11

ACKNOWLEDGMENTS

I thank Hakadosh Baruch Hu for bringing this project to fruition.
I thank my *rebbe*, HaGaon Reb Dovid Feinstein, *shlita*. I have been privileged to learn in his *kollel*, Beth Medrash L'Torah V'Horaah for the last nine years. I was fortunate to discuss with him much of the material covered here. His insightful comments illuminate many of the concepts explored in this work. I would like to thank him for allowing me to ask and re-ask my questions until I felt I understood the concepts clearly. His imprint is present throughout the book, even where I do not quote him by name.

I feel a special need to thank HaGaon Rav Elimelech Bluth, *shlita*, Rav of Congregation Ahavas Achim of Kensington, who makes himself available to guide aspiring *Bnei Torah*. Through his *kollel*, he provides a haven for Torah in Kensington, Brooklyn.

HaGaon Rav Usher David, *shlita*, Rosh Yeshiva of Emek Halachah (Lakewood) has been a tremendous source of inspiration. In addition to the awe I have of his vast Torah knowledge, he constantly encourages me in my researching and writing. In particular, I wish to thank him for reading the entire manuscript, commenting, and writing a *haskomoh*.

I am grateful to HaGaon Rav Yisroel Belsky, *shlita*, Rosh Yeshiva of Yeshiva Torah Vodaas, for kindly reading the manuscript and returning it with many comments. (The text has been amended appropriately.) He also benevolently wrote a *haskomoh*. Thanks are due to his son, Reb Avrohom, for his assistance in these matters.

HaRav Chaim Ganszwieg, *shlita*, Mashgiach of Mesivta Tiferes Jerusalem, kindly reissued an enhanced *haskomoh* in honor of this book.

It is with deep appreciation that I thank HaRav Dovid Goldwasser, *shlita*, Rav of Khal Bnai Yitzchok, for receiving the manuscript so warmly and writing a beautiful preface. Thanks are due to his son-in-law, Reb Chezkey Holtzberg, for his assistance in this matter.

These and other *Rabbanim* took time from their busy schedules to discuss with me the material covered here.

My father, Reb Shimon Reit, *shlita*, through his infectious love of *minhagim*, has inspired me to delve into and research the background of many *minhagim*, including *kaparos*. I am grateful to him for this, as well as for myriad other things.

The work of several people greatly enhanced this volume. They transformed the humdrum into the exciting, and working with them was an extremely enjoyable experience.

I sincerely thank my mother, Mrs. Sara Reit, my father-in-law, Dr. Yehuda Sorscher, and my brother-in-law, Rabbi Ahron Nochum Levi, for their editorial help. Special thanks are due to Mrs. Felice Eisner and Mrs. Reva Leah Rotenfeld who worked on early versions of the manuscript. Mrs. Rotenfeld's thought-provoking comments enhance every page of this work.

The entire staff of Mosaica Press was a pleasure to work with. Rabbi Doron Kornbluth's edit of the manuscript was more thorough than I thought possible. His comments opened up new vistas for me and helped direct my writing to a wider audience. Through his initiation, this book grew by one third. It was a pleasure to work with Rav Yaacov Haber. He was pleasant and insightful. A kindred soul, he understood my needs and was able to provide for them.

I must thank my sons Yosef and Naftali, who helped photograph many of the pictures for this volume. Moshe Gershbaum, of Brilliant Photography, accompanied me to *kaparos* centers to shoot some fantastic pictures amid the tumult and bustle typical of such venues. Shmuel Kaffe once again did a superb job preparing the pictures for print. Rabbi Yitzy Erps's artwork adorns the front cover of this book. He also produced the diagrams, appearing in the section on butchering, depicting how to dissect a chicken.

My dear friend, Rabbi Yechiel Elchanan Rosenblatt, stands out from among the many that have helped. Over the years he assisted with researching and critiquing the project as it moved through its many stages. I am greatly indebted for the beautiful review he wrote about the *Tekufas Hashanah* series.

Since I began this project six years ago, many people shared their information and research with me. Others took the time to read the manuscript, critique and share *ha'aros*. Many of those comments have found their way into the current edition. You all deserve a heartfelt thank you.

May we all be *zocheh* to *teshuvah sheleimah*,

Avrohom Reit

PREFACE

By: HaRav Dovid Goldwasser, shlita

The *minhag* of *kaparos* dates back to the days of the Gaonim. The literal translation of *kaparah* is atonement. The ritual is usually performed Erev Yom Kippur, or during the days leading up to it. Its purpose is to symbolically transfer one's sins to the object used, i.e., a chicken, money, etc., and in that way attain redemption.

The *"shlugging"* of *kaparos* is a once-a-year event that illustrates our quest for atonement, and the details of its observance in different communities have significant meaning to them. Once, when a husband and wife in their first year of marriage disagreed about the fulfillment of *kaparos*, they were so distraught about its proper performance that they sought a *psak* from none other than the *gadol ha-dor*, HaGaon Rav Elazar Menachem Mann Shach.

The Alter of Kelm once happened upon a stone bench as he was taking a walk. Regarding it, he recalled an interesting *medrash* that tells of R' Yehuda finding the rock that R' Meir had sat upon when he learned Torah. R' Yehuda approached the rock and kissed it, comparing it to Har Sinai, the place where the Torah had been given to Klal Yisrael.

The Alter noted that conceptualizing the image of R' Meir's rock could perhaps be understood intellectually. The effectiveness of a visual tangible object such as the stone bench, however, was much more powerful and impressive. The Alter had learned the *medrash* in his youth, but the vision of the stone bench brought the *medrash* to life.

The *Shem M'Shmuel* explains that today's *kaparos* are a physical manifestation of the *sa'ir la'azazel* , which was designated as the agent to "bear" the sins of Klal Yisrael on Yom Kippur, as cited in the Torah (*Vayikra* 16:10). The *minhag* of *kaparos* is a palpable tactile activity that helps us to better understand the significance and awe of the approaching *Yom HaDin*. When one recites "*Zeh chalifasi, zeh temurasi*—This is my exchange, this is my substitute…" it concretizes the concept of atonement, and replicates in small part the activity that was witnessed at the ceremonies of Yom Kippur. This is similar to the Alter's reaction upon seeing a real stone bench and actualizing a *medrash* he had heard.

With this important work, my esteemed colleague, the outstanding *talmid chacham* Rabbi Reit, provides the reader with a learned philosophical Torah understanding of the unique custom of *kaparos*. In addition, he includes a broad gamut of related topics that will be of great interest to many, such as the evolvement of the *minhag* and an in-depth exposition of the *mitzvos* of *kisuy hadam* and *tza'ar ba'al hachaim*.

As the *minhag* of *kaparos* is part of the *teshuvah* process, this *sefer* is particularly significant, since it serves to clarify inaccuracies and false impressions that are sometimes associated with this honored tradition.

It is interesting to note that the *gematriya* of the word *kaparos* is 706, equivalent to "*Yehei na davar zeh karov el libam*—May this matter be close to their heart." It is my belief that the publication of this *sefer* will create a *chibah yeseirah* for this *minhag*.

I am confident that this *sefer* will be well-received, and will inspire the *klal* to an even higher level of *teshuvah*. I wish the author much *hatzlachah* in all of his efforts *l'hagdil Torah ul'haadirah*. May he be *zocheh* to be counted among the *matzdikei ha-rabbim she'tzidkasam omedes lo'ad*.

המצפה לישועת ה',

Rabbi Dovid Goldwasser

INTRODUCTION

The *minhag* of *kaparos* has great depth of meaning and is based on lofty ideals, yet most people know little about it. There are even adults, who—like pre-schoolers— believe that we are transferring our *aveiros* onto a chicken! Ignorance breeds apathy.

Awareness of the ideas behind the *minhag* would imbue people with a zest for it — and all *minhagim*. After all, an informed consumer is the best consumer.

If you know where to look, there is a tremendous wealth of knowledge available about *kaparos*. However, all the material is scattered among many *sefarim*. There is not one full-length *sefer* that covers the various dimensions of this awe-inspiring *minhag*.

I believe the present work is the first attempt to gather the many concepts of *kaparos* into one cohesive read. By reading a variety of sources, I was able to view the *minhag* from several perspectives. I have attempted to fuse this material together into a very readable, comprehensible and comprehensive text. The current work sheds light on many aspects of the *minhag* not often covered in the articles designed to explain the custom. It is my hope that through education people will be galvanized to relate to the *minhag* appropriately.

In preparing this book, I had to translate many sources and quotes. I tried to translate literally while retaining the flavor and expressive beauty of the poetry of *Tanach* and *Chazal*. In a similar vein, I tried to present the words of the *Rishonim* in Standard English while preserving their full meaning. I hope the reader will find my translations accurate and enjoyable.

Although this volume is based on numerous *sefarim*, each of which adds a few details to the big picture, I have tried not to burden the reader with long lists of sources. If I would cite all the ideas included in the current work, there would be more footnotes than text! Whenever possible I tried to list just one reference in the notes. As a rule, I limited myself to the most accessible and easiest-to-locate *sefer*. If you find that my language does not exactly match that of the attributed source, most likely there were other *Acharonim* who expressed this idea with a different twist.

As a convenience for the reader, a list of the main texts upon which this work is based, as well as many of the harder-to-locate *sefarim*, is appended at the end of this volume.

This book is consumer-oriented. It focuses on the real-life *kaparos* setup found in most modern cities. Both the textual descriptions and pictorial depictions will reflect the scene at your local *kaparos* center. For this reason we opted to use "backyard" or "RealFeel" pictures. We hoped to project the typical commercial *kaparos* scene and the home *kashering* environment.

I found writing this book to be a true pleasure. Researching the sources and contemplating the information was both fascinating and illuminating. I hope you will feel the same way!

OVERVIEW

Part One: A Minhag

But it's just a *minhag*. Why make such a big deal out of it?

This work is about just one *minhag—kaparos*. However, before we move on to our main topic, a word about *minhagim* in general is in order. Consider: Why do *minhagim* even exist? Why were they preserved though the generations?

Minhagim fall into two broad categories: *halachic* and *hashkafic*. (These can be subdivided further, but that is beyond the scope of this work.)

The first category, *halachic*, can be described simply as the manner in which we do a mitzvah. If there is a *machlokes* regarding how to perform a mitzvah, for example, a *minhag* would reflect one of the points of view. Whether you stand or sit for *kiddush* would be an expression of halachic *minhag*.

Hashkafic minhagim are a broad topic. We will focus on just one aspect—the *minhagim* that are the spice that invigorates our performance of *mitzvos*. These *minhagim* breathe life into our *Yiddishkeit*. They help imbue us with a sense of what *Yiddishkeit* is all about. They are responsible, in part, for the beautiful and directed life of the Torah Jew.

Without *minhagim*, practical Shabbos would be a day of restrictions. With them, we have a *seudah*. We sing *zemiros*. The foods we eat and the songs we sing create an atmosphere that brings out the beauty and *kedushah* of Shabbos.

No doubt, *minhagim* set the tone and bring the mitzvah to life. Without them, our mitzvah performance would be cold and commonplace. Imagine the *Yamim Noraim* without *selichos*, Yom Kippur without *Kol Nidrei* or a *kittel*! How different Purim would be if there were no costumes! And Chanukah would not be the same without *latkes*!

Minhagim are not merely the practices adopted and adapted by the masses. They are founded by our great leaders for *halachic* and *hashkafic* reasons. They are intended to solve *halachic* dilemmas or teach lessons of *hashkafah*. Imbedded in them is as much depth and logic as one would expect of people of such caliber.

Many *minhagim* were instituted by *Chazal* and are mentioned in the Gemara. *Hallel* on Rosh Chodesh,[1] *Hoshanos* on Hoshanah Rabbah,[2] and *selichos* on a fast day,[3] are just a few. Other *minhagim*, like *Kol Nidrei*[4] and *Simchas Torah*[5] have their origins in the time of the *Geonim*. Signing a letter with the words, "*L'shanah tovah tekasev,*" is an example of a *minhag* begun in the period of the *Rishonim*.[6] There are even *minhagim* that began in later generations, like those started by the Arizal.

But, can a *minhag* really have so many rules and particulars?

---

1   *Tanis* 28b.
2   *Succah* 42a, *et al.*
3   *Tanis* 14a, *Rashi* s.v. *Rav Yehudah.*
4   *Tur* §619, citing Rav Sa'adyah Gaon.
5   *Beis Yosef,* §339:3.
6   *Maharil, Yamim Noraim* 3.

Definitely! As matter of fact, there are many *simanim* in *Shulchan Aruch* dedicated just to the details of *minhagim*. The very first *siman* in *Shulchan Aruch* is almost entirely about *minhagim*. *Simanim* 131 and 134 about *Tachanun* are exclusively about a *minhag*. A significant part of *hilchos aveilos*, as well all the rules of *Kaddish* and *yahrtzeit*, are *minhagim*.

Furthermore, one *minhag* may be designed to solve several concerns. Details may be added to cover many angles. To accomplish these, a *minhag* must be profound and multi-faceted.

Kaparos, as we will demonstrate in Chapter One, dates to the time of *Chazal*. Sanctioned by the greats of every subsequent generation, the *minhag* contains a wealth of lessons and beauty. It behooves us to study the *minhag* as befits the enactments of men of such stature.

MEANING OF THE WORD KAPARAH

CLEANSE

אכפרה פניו - אבטל רוגזו וכו' ונראה בעיני שכל כפרה שאצל עון וחטא ואצל פנים כולן לשון קנוח והעברה הן, ולשון ארמי הוא הרבה בתלמוד וכפר ידיה (ב"מ כד א), בעי לכפורי ידיה בההוא גברא (גיטין נו א), וגם בלשון המקרא נקראים המזרקים של קדש (עזרא א י) כפורי זהב, על שם שהכהן מקנח ידיו בהן בשפת המזרק (רש"י בראשית לב:כא):

REPLACE

כתוב בישעיה (מג:ג) כִּי אֲנִי ה' אלקיך קָדוֹשׁ יִשְׂרָאֵל מוֹשִׁיעֶךָ נָתַתִּי כָפְרְךָ מִצְרַיִם כּוּשׁ וּסְבָא תַּחְתֶּיךָ: ופירוש רש"י - נתתי כפרך מצרים - והם היו לך לפדיון שבכוריהם מתו ואתה בני בכורי נצלת והייתם חייבים כליה כמו שנאמר (ביחזקאל כ) ואומר לשפוך חמתי עליהם בארץ מצרים:

COVER

ועשית כפרת - כדמות מכסה, ואמר יפת, כי כמוהו לכפר עליו (ויקרא א, ד), כמו כסוי חטאה (תהלים לב, א). ולפי דעתי, שמלת לכפר עליו, כגזרת כופר. והנה זה מפורש, ונתנו איש כפר נפשו (שמות ל, יב). ושם כתוב לכפר על נפשותיכם (שם, טו): ר"ל שהכופר מכסה עליו ומגין עליו מחטאיו. (אבן עזרא שמות כה:יז):

Part Two: The Name

The *minhag* is called *kaparos*—כפרות, the chicken is called a *kaparah*—כפרה, and the day is called (Yom) Kippur—(יום) כפור. They all obviously share a common Hebrew root. What does this word mean?

The root כפר and its derivatives appear many times throughout *Tanach*. In *Tanach*, the root has three primary meanings. It can mean to cleanse, to replace, and to cover. In the accompanying box on the previous page, I provide one prime example from *Tanach* of how it is used in each sense.[7]

All three meanings of this root are reflected in the *minhag*. When we do *kaparos*, we *cleanse* our souls through *teshuvah*, the chicken *replaces* our bodies for punishment, and the ritual *covers* and shields us from harm. (These themes will be developed throughout the book.)

Why haven't I included "atone" as one of its meanings? Certainly, that is the most common translation of the word. Still, I am looking for its truest sense, the way it appears in *Tanach* and the way the *Rishonim* were likely to have used it. In these sources, *kaper* is not used to express "atonement." According to my dictionary, atone means "to turn away from sin or do penitence." Penitence is then defined as "remorse for your past conduct." These words seem to define *teshuvah* more than כפר.

Since the times of *Tanach*, the word *kaper* has stretched. It has now come to include atone. (And the word atone has also stretched. It is used colloquially, even in this book, to mean forgiveness.) I don't know anybody who would *not* translate Yom Kippur as the Day of Atonement. In many *sefarim*, as well as in Yiddish, the word *kaparah* is also used as a synonym for chicken. Many *machzorim* give instructions to, "Take the *kaparah*." Throughout this work, we too, will use the modern and Yiddish connotations of this word.

Subtleties of language aside, one thing is clear. *Kaparos* is a *minhag* designed to draw us closer to *teshuvah sheleimah*, and to the forgiveness and protection that come as a result.

---

7   See also *Radak's Sharashim* under the entry "כפר."

CHAPTER ONE

The Origins: The earliest sources for the custom

Waving a chicken over one's head for *kaparos* is certainly an unusual *minhag*. There isn't anything even remotely similar among the rest of our lifecycle customs. Yet, as *minhagim* go, *kaparos* is among the oldest. The earliest explicit discussion about *kaparos* is in *Teshuvos HaGeonim*,[8] compiled approximately one thousand years ago, where it is mentioned in three *teshuvos*.[9] However, there are indications that it was already practiced in the time of the Gemara.

Although the custom is not mentioned outright anywhere in the Talmud, there is evidence that it was an accepted practice in that era. In *Maseches Shabbos*,[10] the Gemara states that it is permitted to move an item called פרפיסא—*parfisa*—on Shabbos. Rashi, quoting *Teshuvos HaGeonim*, explains that *parfisa* was a potted plant used to perform a *kaparos*-like ceremony for children on Erev Rosh Hashanah. In effect, Rashi is saying that some form of *kaparos* was practiced in the time of *Chazal*.[11]

Kaparos is also alluded to in *Maseches Chullin*,[12] where the Gemara talks about many livers, kidneys, and udders that had been discarded in the streets on Erev Yom Kippur.

---

8   *Teshuvos HaGeonim* is a collection of *halachic* responsa authored by a group of Babylonian Talmudic scholars between the years 4350 (589 c.e.) and 4800 (1040 c.e.).

9   שערי תשובה רצ״ט, תשובות הגאונים החדשות - עמנואל (אופק) סימן י, תשובות הגאונים - מוסאפיה (ליק) סימן ח. These *teshuvos* can be found in the appendix ב, ג, ד.

10 81b.

11 This *Rashi* appears in the Appendix ה. It will be quoted and explained on page 58, "Plants and Chickens."

12 95b; 110a.

The Rosh and other *mefarshim*[13] explain that the local *Yidden* slaughtered their *kaparos* animals and discarded their innards in accordance with the *minhag*.[14]

There is a possible third ancient source for the *minhag*. The *Machzor Vitri*[15] opens the topic of *kaparos* with the following words:

סדר של יום הכיפורים, מנהג אבותינו תורה היא, וכך היא בפסיקתא, ערב יום הכיפורים מביאין תרנגולין וכו'.

> *The schedule for Yom Kippur: The customs of our fathers are [authentic] Torah, and so is it in the Peskita, on the eve of Yom Kippur chickens are brought…*

The word *Pesikta* here seems to be a reference to the *medrash* by that name.

It appears that the *Machzor Vitri* had such a *medrash* and that he is using it as a source for the *minhag*. We, however, do not have such a quote in our version of the *medrash*. The words "On the eve of Yom Kippur chickens are brought…" do not appear anywhere in the extant version. While this may weaken the credibility of the *medrash* it does not totally discount it. The *Rishonim* often quote passages of *medrash* that have not been preserved to our day.

It should be noted that the concept of an animal taking the place of a person—a theme central to *kaparos*, as will be elaborated on below—does appear in the *Pesikta*:

א"ר יצחק בנוהג שבעולם אדם נכשל בעבירה והוא מתחייב עליה מיתה לשמים, מת שורו, אבדה תרנגולתו, נשברה צלוחיתו, ניכשל באצבעו, מקצת הנפש ככל הנפש.[16]

---

13   See *Rosh* to *Yoma* §8:23, quoted in *Tur* 605.

14   The purpose of discarding the organs into the street is addressed on page 56, "Discarding the Innards."

15   §339.

16   *Pesikta D'Rav Kahanah* (24)—*Shuvah*.

Rabbi Yitzchak said, "It would be expected that if a person sinned, he should be castigated with capital punishment. If his ox dies, his chicken is lost, his pitcher breaks or he injures a finger—part of the soul is like the entire soul [i.e., the loss of the item has excused him].[17]

Even if we discount this third source as unverified, the Gemara in *Maseches Shabbos* as explained by Rashi and the Gemaros in *Maseches Chullin* as explained by the Rosh provide us with two Talmudic sources for *kaparos*. The three *Teshuvos HaGeonim* provide us with additional ancient sources.

In the coming chapters we will cover this *minhag* from many angles. We will discuss the rationale behind the *minhag* in general, as well as the logic behind each of its many details. Included are instructions on how to do *kaparos* that you will not find in any *machzor* (from how to hold a chicken to the laws of *kisuy hadam*) and advice on what to do with your chicken after *kaparos*. Finally, we will explain the *pesukim* recited during *kaparos*, providing context for the *pesukim* based on their sources.

Let's begin by talking about an ancient debate among the *Rishonim* as to whether *kaparos* is permissible.

---

17   Perhaps we can suggest an alternate reading of the *Machzor Vitri*: Besides being the name of a *medrash*, *pesikta* can also mean, "with certainty." Thus, it is possible that the *Machzor Vitri* is not referring to the *medrash* at all. Instead he is using the word in its other connotation, with certainty. The opening phrase— מנהג אבותינו תורה היא—could be explained to be a response to those who questioned the authenticity of this *minhag*. (This will be further addressed below.) Without verbalizing the question or explaining the answer, the *Machzor Vitri* starts the discussion with the declaration, "[All] our traditions are unquestionable and this is indisputable…"Whether the *Machzor Vitri* affords us a third source has no bearing on the credibility of the previous two sources.

CHAPTER TWO

THE *KAPAROS* DEBATE:
THE ADVOCATES AND THE DISSENTERS AMONG THE *RISHONIM*

Kaparos is mentioned in almost every halachah and *minhag sefer* and appears to have been universal. Most *Rishonim* accepted and even defended the *minhag*.[18] However, the Ramban and Rashba[19] spoke out against *kaparos*, describing it as *darkei ha'emori*—an *avodah zarah*-style custom[20]—and tried to put an end to it.[21]

Darkei ha'emori literally means the "ways of the Emorites" (i.e., pagans). It is a generic term that covers a range of forbidden, gentile-like activities. In particular, those that are thought to produce supernatural results.[22] All the various forms of divining, auspice, necromancy and thaumaturgy fall under this heading. Included also would be the search for omens.

---

18   The list of *Rishonim* in favor is too long to cite. We will suffice with just a few of the most readily available *sefarim*: *Rosh, Yoma* 23; *Mordechai, Yoma* 723; *Tur* 605; *Machzor Vitri* 339; *Shibbolei Haleket* 283; *Maharil, Erev Yom Kippur* 2.

19   *Shu"t Rashba* 1:395.

20   The definition in the text is based on *Darkei Moshe Yoreh De'ah* §178:1. The *Rishonim* quoted in the *Beis Yosef loc. cit.* might describe *darkei ha'emori* as—nonsensical habit.

21   The *Meiri* in *Chibur Hateshuvah* (2:8, page 398) is not in favor of *kaparos*. He is not listed here because a) he is not quoted by the *Beis Yosef* or any of the *Acharonim*, b) he does not forbid the custom, he only says it would be preferred if people wouldn't do it. If it is obvious that the practitioner's intention is for the Sake of Heaven (see page 47 "*Pesukim*," for the *Meiri's* suggestion), he does not oppose it.

22   *Shabbos* 67a, and *Tosefta Shabbos* Chp. 6–7.

Actions that can be understood logically[23] or have been proven effective through trial and error are allowed.[24] The use of artifacts or actions that are unproven or have no simple explanation are considered *darkei ha'emori*.[25]

(*Simanim*, by way of contrast, are permissible.[26] *Simanim* are actions or events that people interpret as indicants of past or future good tidings. These are allowed since the person does not rely on or place his trust in them. Their function is only to make the person feel good, plan his future, or commence in a good manner.[27] A familiar example would be the *simanim* we eat as part of the Rosh Hashanah meal. We will see later[28] that *kaparos* may also be viewed in this light).

The Rashba felt that waving a chicken overhead to effect atonement fell into the category of the forbidden. He writes,[29]

> …That you saw [read] that I forbade the *kaparos* done for the youth on Erev Yom Kippur… This was among many customs widespread in our city that I thought to be *darkei ha'emori*. They would *shecht* an old rooster to atone for a recently born lad. They would sever the head and hang the feather-draped head, along with garlic, over the door… Although I heard from very reliable people that in Ashkenaz they *shecht* geese and chickens on Erev Yom Kippur for *kaparos* and that Rav Hai Gaon authenticated the *minhag*, I terminated the custom.

---

23   *Aruch Hashulchan O.C.* §301:80.

24   Ibid. and *Mishnah Berurah* §301:105.

25   Ibid.

26   *Yoreh De'ah* 179:2.

27   See *Rambam, Avodah Zarah* 11:4-5 and *Kesef Mishnah* there. The topic of *darkei ha'emori* and its peripherals are extensive and scattered all over *Shas* and the *poskim*. Use the sources cited as a springboard for further study.

28   Page 40, "Inaugurating the New Year"; page 52, "When to Perform the *Minhag*."

29   *Shu"t Rashba* 1:395.

It should be noted that the Rashba's description of the custom practiced in his city seems radically different than *kaparos* as it is described by any of the other *Rishonim* or anything in practice today. Nonetheless, since the Rashba opens with a mention of *kaparos* on Erev Yom Kippur, the Beis Yosef[30] cites the Rashba as forbidding the custom altogether.[31]

In *Shulchan Aruch*, Rav Yosef Karo agreed with the Rashba[32] and wrote that the *minhag* should be abolished.[33]

The Rama defended the *minhag*, calling it "the custom of the devout."

The *minhag* as practiced in the Rashba's region did not include giving the chicken or its value to the poor. The Radvaz[34] postulates that even the Rashba would have permitted the custom if the chickens had been donated to *tzedakah* as is done today, since requesting life and prosperity in exchange for *tzedakah* is neither inappropriate nor regarded as sorcery. The Radvaz bases this on a statement in the Gemara:[35] "האומר סלע זו לצדקה בשביל שיחיו בני... הרי זו צדיק גמור—One who says 'This *selah*-coin shall be for

---

30   §605.

31   See also Rav M.M. Kasher, *Divrei Menachem, Yom Kippur* 18 (appendix לא) and Rav M. M. Karp, *Hilchos Chag B'chag, Yamim Noraim* p. 275.

32   The *Shulchan Aruch* states simply, "The *minhag* should be abolished," and stops short of calling it *darkei ha'emori*. This has led some contemporary writers to speculate about the rationale behind this ruling. Nevertheless, it is safe to assume that this statement is based on the Rashba's *teshuvah*, since it is the Rashba who is quoted in the *Beis Yosef* as the opposing opinion. In addition, the wording of the *Shulchan Aruch* is paraphrased from the Rashba's writings. (See *Mishnah Berurah* §605:1.)

33   The first several editions of *Shulchan Aruch* had a chapter heading that read, "מנהג כפרות בערב יום כפור מנהג של שטות הוא — The Custom of Kaparos Performed on Erev Yom Kippur is a Foolish Custom." It has been debated whether the Mechaber himself could have written this or if it was added by an antagonistic printer. Later printers found this phrase offensive and deleted the words "מנהג של שטות הוא."

34   *Shu"t Radvaz* 2:740.

35   *Rosh Hashanah* 4a, and see *Bava Basra* 10b.

tzedakah in order that my sons survive,' is a genuine *tzaddik*." If giving *tzedakah* in order to gain merit is praiseworthy, then donating chickens to the poor to obtain merit can be easily justified.

(According to this understanding, the emphasis of *kaparos* would be on the charity aspect. The ceremony of the chicken would be simply to symbolically connect the merit of the *tzedakah* to the participant.[36])

Even when the chickens were not donated to the poor, the vast majority of *Rishonim* and *Acharonim* did not consider *kaparos* to be sorcery. They understood the custom is intended to arouse the participant to *teshuvah*, and does not mysteriously and supernaturally, in and of itself, affect *kaparah*. When the chickens are given to the less fortunate, as is done today, it is likely that even the Rashba would permit the *minhag*.

All the *sefarim* that debate whether *kaparos* falls under the prohibition of *darkei ha'emori* deal only with chickens. That is because until recently only chickens were used for *kaparos*. It is important to note that according to those who forbade *kaparos*, money would also be included in the ban. Waving coins overhead, or even "transferring one's essence" onto a coin, is no less the practice of thaumaturgy than doing so with chickens.[37] The use of coins for *kaparos* would be no different than the use of grasshopper eggs and fox teeth. (The Gemara[38] forbids wearing grasshopper eggs and fox teeth when not for medicinal gain.)

---

36   These topics will be elaborated on in the coming chapters. See page 73, "Tzedakah," and page 77, "Money," about the role of charity. See chap. 4 about connecting the "*kaparah*" to the penitent.

37   Based on *Pri Chadash* §605. In his discussion about *kaparos* he mentions the use of both chickens and plants (see below page 58 "Plants and Chickens"). In his conclusion he discourages the use of both as *darkei ha'emori*. There is no reason to assume that money is any less of an issue.

38   *Shabbos* 67a.

Today, *kaparos* is practiced throughout the Jewish world. This is due to the benefits of the *minhag*, its canonization by the Rama, its sanction by the vast majority of the *Rishonim*, and its ratification by the *Acharonim*. Even the *Sefardim*, who ordinarily follow the Mechaber, perform it. This is probably because of the influence of the Arizal, who was a strong advocate of the *minhag*.[39]

---

39   Quoted in *Magen Avraham* §605:1.

CHAPTER THREE

KAPAROS, THE RATIONALE: AN EXPOSITION OF THE *MINHAG*

Why do *kaparos*? Previously we established that it is an ancient custom and is not considered *darkei ha'emori*. Now we will address the purpose and intended benefits of the *minhag*.

To appreciate a custom one must understand the rationale behind it—why it was established and what lessons it is supposed to convey. In this chapter we will explore the six reasons given for the *minhag* of *kaparos*. These ideas—the *korban* connection, substitution, distraction, inauguration, blessing, and *Akeidah*—are found in the *Rishonim* and *Acharonim* that talk about *kaparos*. Hopefully, a thorough understanding of the background and basis of the *minhag* will give us an appreciation for the custom and its many aspects.

1. **The *kaparos-korban* connection:**

Two aspects of *korbanos* are represented in *kaparos*: (a) repentance and (b) forgiveness.

> a.   In the era of the Beis HaMikdash, a person who, through his sins, distanced himself from Hakadosh Baruch Hu was able to bring an animal as a *korban*. It was a part of the *teshuvah* process. When bringing a *korban* and watching the animal go to its death, the person realized that his misdeeds were destructive. According to strict justice, it is he, not the animal, who should have been dismembered and had his limbs placed on the *mizbe'ach*. Through this heightened awareness achieved

by bringing a *korban*, a person can be brought to *teshuvah*. By offering an animal, a living being so similar to himself whose organs are now on the *mizbe'ach*, he feels as though he has given himself over to Hakadosh Baruch Hu.[40]

Watching the *shechitah* of the *kaparos*-chicken should, like a *korban*, arouse the person to *teshuvah*. *Kaparos* thus developed as a *teshuvah* program very similar to a *korban*. *Kaparos*, like a *korban*, included *viduy*, *semichah*, and *shechitah*.[41]

b.   The second dimension of a *korban* is forgiveness. When a person who has done *teshuvah* brings a *korban*, Hashem forgives his sins. It is our hope that through the *korban*-like process of *kaparos*, we too will achieve *teshuvah* and forgiveness of our sins.

Korbanos also teach us that thoughts alone are never enough. Even the loftiest thought is still "just a thought" until it is translated into action. Only through action can a person prove his convictions. The thoughts of *teshuvah* and remorse the penitent experiences, as important as they are, are still just thoughts. A *korban* is required to help concretize the thoughts and feelings of repentance.[42]

Similarly, the yearning and the thoughts of *teshuvah* a person may be feeling at this time of the year must yet be translated into something concrete. Just as the *korban* process demonstrates his submission to Hakadosh Baruch Hu, the act of *kaparos* attests to his *teshuvah*.[43]

---

40   *Darkei Moshe* §605:3. This concept is the basic idea behind *korbanos*. The way it is expressed here is based on the writings of the *Ramban* and *Rabbenu B'chai* in the beginning of *Sefer Vayikra* (1:9). (For the reader's convenience these works have been appended to this volume, Appendix כה, כו.) *Darkei Moshe* explains that *kaparos* parallels *korbanos* in this respect.

41   These concepts will be elaborated on in chap. 4, see page 43.

42   Based on *Ramban, Vayikra* 1:9.

43   See also *Otzar Hatefillos, Tikun Tefillah* toward the end.

2. Substitution:[44]

On one of his travels, Rabbi Akiva tried to find lodgings in a town. All the locals refused him and he was forced to spend the night in the forest. He comforted himself that at least he had his donkey, rooster and candle. Unfortunately, a lion soon ate his donkey, a cat killed the rooster, a wind extinguished his candle, and he was left alone in the dark. During the night, gangs attacked the town and took all the inhabitants captive, but Rabbi Akiva was spared.[45]

The Maharal[46] learns a fascinating concept from this story: A person's animal can stand in his place if he is decreed to die. Indeed, it was through the death of his rooster, called *gever* in Hebrew, from the same root that means "man," that Rabbi Akiva's own life was saved.

A similar lesson can be learned from a different story in the Gemara.

Nechunya the cistern digger regularly prepared wells for the benefit of the *olay regel*— the holiday pilgrims. Nechunya's daughter once fell into a large water pit. Twice, Rebbe Chanina ben Dosa was approached to pray for her, and twice he assured the people that she will yet emerge. When enough time had elapsed that it was no longer possible for her to survive under water, he informed the people she must

---

44   *Korbanos* also have a dimension of substitution (i.e., the animal standing for the person). Regarding *korbanos* the connection to the penitent is obvious and takes place on the *mizbe'ach*. Here the relationship to the redeemed is remote and occurs outside of the Beis HaMikdash.

45   *Berachos* 60b. The conclusion of the story is well-known. The Gemara tells, as each seeming misfortune happened, Rebbe Akiva uttered his famous maxim, "*Gam zu l'tovah*—This too is for the best." The end of the story proved that Rebbe Akiva was right. The town's inhabitants were led away and he was spared.

46   נתיב הבטחון פ' א' (דפוס יהדות דף רלג), נתיב אהבת ה' פ' א' (דפוס יהדות דף מב).
The text of the Maharal appears in Appendix יט.

have surely emerged. When the rescuers found her, they asked, "How did you get out?" She replied, "A ram—the ram of Yitzchak—led by an elderly man—Avraham Avinu—rescued me."[47]

The Pnei Yehoshua[48] explains that it is clear that she was saved through the prayers of Rebbe Chanina ben Dosa.[49] What then was the role of the ram? Since it had been decreed for her to die, it was now necessary to substitute something—Yitzchak's ram—in her stead, in order for her to survive.

It is for this reason, continues the Pnei Yehoshua, that people use a chicken on Erev Yom Kippur to perform *kaparos*. In case it had been decreed for someone to die, the chicken will stand in his place. This is similar to the incident at the *Akeidah* in which Yitzchak himself was replaced by the ram.

In explaining the rationale for *kaparos*, the Mahari Veil[50] express a similar idea:

> This is the meaning of the *pasuk*, "The tzaddik is delivered from harm; the evil one relieves him."[51] It is also written, "He was rescued from going to the grave, a replacement was found."[52] Once the destructive angel has set out, he does not return [rest] until he has accomplished his mission in some way…

---

47   *Bava Kama* 50a.

48   Ibid.

49   Rebbe Chanina ben Dosa was renowned for his ability to daven on behalf of people. See *Berachos* 34b and *Tanis* 24b.

50   *Teshuvos Mahari Veil* 191. The text of the *Mahari Veil* appears in Appendix ח׳.

51   *Mishlei* 11:8.

52   *Iyov* 33:24.

The Satan, by nature, must fulfill his mission of destruction. If he cannot carry it out in the manner planned, he will do so in whatever way he can.[53] (Actually, there are many other places where *Chazal* say the loss of a person's animal can excuse him from punishment [e.g., *Pesachim* 118a, *Yalkut Shimoni, Hoshea* 533]).[54]

According to this reasoning, the *kaparah* does not serve as a prompt to *teshuvah* nor does it aid in forgiving one's sins. Rather, the death of the chicken can be substituted as the fulfillment of an unfavorable decree against the person.

3. Distraction:

Kaparos provides the Satan with a diversion, in order to prevent him from carrying out a harsh sentence against a person. In the time of the Beis HaMikdash, as part of the Yom Kippur *avodah*, a young, male goat was thrown from a cliff. This goat, called the *sa'ir hameshtale'ach*, was thrown from a cliff outside of Yerushalayim. *Pirkei D'Rebbe Eliezer*[55] describes the *sa'ir hameshtale'ach* as a lure to distract the Satan from interfering with the favorable judgment of the *tzaddikim* on Yom Kippur. Thus, *kaparos* plays a role similar to the role of the *sa'ir hameshtale'ach* that was part of the Yom Kippur *Avodah* in the Beis HaMikdash.[56]

---

53   This idea also appears in the Gemara *Chagigah* 4b, מרים מגדל שער נשים. In some of these cases (the Gemara Chagigah, Mahari Veil and the Pnei Yehoshua), it was not necessary for the substitution item to be in any way connected to the person which it replaces.

54   This is not to be confused with a similar but different concept. Hashem first tries to prod a person to *teshuvah* by punishing him though his possessions before attempting to punish the person directly (e.g., *Yalkut Shimoni, Shemini* 563).

55   Chap. 46. See *Ramban, Vayikra* 1:9 for an elaboration of this theme.

56   *Levush* §605. The connection to *sa'ir hameshtale'ach* is made by several *Rishonim*, (*Machzor Vitri* 339, *Tzedah Laderech, mamar* 4, *klal* 5). According to the Arizal it is the primary purpose of *kaparos*.

4. Inaugurating the new year:

There is a popular custom based on the Gemara[57] of inaugurating the new year by eating the special *simanim* foods. The purpose of the custom is to start the year with symbols of blessing. These foods, eaten during the Rosh Hashanah evening *seudah*, represent concepts and ideals that Jews hold dear. An apple, for example, symbolizing the Jewish people, is dipped in honey which represents sweetness; a pomegranate characterizes multitudes of *mitzvos*; a fish connotes being fruitful and multiplying; a head of an animal signifies leadership. These foods, as well as being omens for a good future, actually set the tone and begin the year in an auspicious manner.

In a similar way, enacting the *kaparos* ceremony starts the year on a positive note. It commences the year with a symbol of blessing—in this case, *kaparah*, or atonement. Doing so helps ensure that the coming year will be one in which Hashem will forgive His people.[58]

According to this reasoning, the ideal time to perform the ceremony would be on Erev Rosh Hashanah. These important symbols of *berachah* would then be in place by the time the new year begins. And indeed, the *Rishonim* who suggest this reason also say to do it then. However, even according to our custom to do it before Yom Kippur, we can still achieve this goal. This is because the days from the beginning of Tishrei through Yom Kippur are all considered the "beginning of the year."

5. Blessing:

In Talmudic times, chickens were considered a sign of fertility. Birds and fish were especially blessed on the fifth day of Creation to "be fruitful and multiply."[59]

---

57   *Horeius* 12b.
58   *Shibbolei HaLeket* 283, *Darkei Moshe* §605:1.
59   *Bereshis* 1:22.

Therefore, chickens were often paraded at the head of a wedding procession[60] to signify that the new couple should be fertile. Chickens were chosen for this role, because, as noted above, the Hebrew word for rooster—*gever*—also means man.[61]

At the onset of the new year, a time when we make so many other requests, we include a request that the members of our family, along with all of Klal Yisrael, be fruitful and multiply.[62] The chicken is eaten later. Like the other *simanim* consumed on Rosh Hashanah, our *minhag* is to eat the symbolic foods.

6. *Akeidah*/**Mutual love:**

There was an ancient *minhag* to use a ram for *kaparos* in order to remember the *Akeidah*. The *Avos*, Avraham and Yitzchak, demonstrated their immense love for Hakadosh Baruch Hu through the *Akeidah*. In return, Hashem promised to always remember Klal Yisrael with love. Through *kaparos*, we call attention to this mutual love.[63]

What we have discovered:

Kaparos is an offshoot of *korbanos*; its practice was influenced by the power of a *korban* to bring people to *teshuvah* and elicit forgiveness. *Kaparos* is also rooted in the notion that a person's animal or belongings can stand in his place if punishment is due him, in the concept of "distracting the Satan," in the value of *simanei berachah* to inaugurate a new

---

60   *Gittin* 57a.
61   See *Maharsha* ibid.
62   See *Biur HaGra* §605:4.
63   *Tur* §605.

time or new venture, or to evoke the *zechus* of a pivotal time of connection to Hashem such as the *Akeidah*.

These are the ideas upon which the *minhag* was founded. As we read the next chapter, we will learn the role these reasons played in the development of different aspects of the custom. We will reference these themes and build on them. We will also discuss why some aspects of the *minhag* are no longer practiced.

CHAPTER FOUR

THE STORY OF — AND AN EXPOSITION OF — KAPAROS

The Development of Kaparos from Ancient Times until Today

Today, the *minhag* of *kaparos* is to wave a chicken around your head several times while saying a few *pesukim* from the *machzor*. It wasn't always that way. A cursory reading of the *Rishonim* reveals that, historically, various places had different *minhagim*:

- In some eras, people used sheep and calves or plants instead of birds.

- There were places where someone other than the penitent read the verses.

- Depending on the locale, different verses were recited before and during the ceremony.

- In some communities, the *minhag* was limited to children, and in others only to male children.

- Some people were careful to *shecht* the animal immediately after the ceremony and some were not.

- Some *shechted* only at night and some waited for morning.

- There were places where they ate the *kaparah* themselves and places where it was distributed to the poor.

- Some communities ate the slaughtered animal at the *seudah* on Erev Yom Kippur and others did not.

- Some were scrupulous to use a white chicken, while others objected to the idea.

- Almost all sources give the time as Erev Yom Kippur, though a few say it was done on Erev Rosh Hashanah.

Although there was diversity in many of the nuances of the *minhag*, all communities were unified in the fundamental idea—to connect an animal to the person—and then *shecht* it.

We will dedicate this chapter to explaining these variations, the details of the *minhag* and the rationale behind them.

Symbolizing a *Korban*

As mentioned earlier, the original *minhag* was designed to resemble a *korban*, complete with *viduy, semichah,* and *shechitah.*[64] One bringing a *korban* is expected to think, "Because of my sins, I deserve to die." When he watches the *shechitah*, he thinks, "This should have happened to me." As he watches the *Kohen* sprinkle the blood and place the fats on the *mizbe'ach*, he thinks, "This should have been me." As he eats the meat of his *korban*, he thinks that Hashem, in His graciousness, has not only allowed him to live, but has even provided him with meat to eat, and he is overcome with thoughts of *teshuvah*.

64   *Tur* §605.

The idea of *kaparos* is similar. The penitent should feel as if he deserves to die because of his sins, and as if the *kaparos*-animal is taking his place. As he watches the slaughtering and thinks, "This is what should have happened to me," he realizes the extent of his sins and is aroused to do a complete *teshuvah*.

In keeping with the concept of *korbanos*—which, in some cases, would vary according to the wealth of those who brought them[65]—there was a *minhag* at one time for rich people to use calves or sheep for *kaparos*,[66] for people with lower incomes to use birds, and for the poorest people to use plants.[67]

The *poskim* found this strong resemblance to *korbanos* disturbing because it might seem to the participant as if he were bringing an actual *korban* outside of the Beis HaMikdash. They therefore tried to minimize the connection. In particular, they objected to the use of sheep and other animals commonly used as *korbanos*, the practice of *semichah*, and the use of the word *temurah*, a term which is often associated with actual *korbanos*. *Chas v'shalom* that one should assume that anybody intended *kaparos* to be a *korban*. Yet, the severity of the *issur* of *shechutei chutz*—offering a *korban* outside of the Beis HaMikdash—compelled the *Acharonim* to take a stance against

---

65   E.g., *Olah V'yored, Keresus* 10b; *Olas R'eyah* and *Shalmei Chagigah, Rambam, Hilchos Chagigah* 1:2, 11.

66   Since the *Rishonim* only mention this custom in passing without providing any details, it can be assumed that it had already fallen out of practice by their time. (See also *Siddur Rav Yacov Emden—Ya'avetz*.) It seems that they did *semichah* by placing their hands on the head of the animal, to replicate a *korban*. The strong parallel to a *korban* alarmed the *Rabbanim* and led them to protest the use of animals and put a halt on *semichah*. The elimination of *semichah* eventually devolved into waving a bird overhead, as will be explained below.

67   This is a synthesis of two *teshuvos* of the *Geonim*. One, quoted by the *Mordechai* (*Yoma* §723), tells that *Rabbanim* and ordinary people used chickens and the wealthy used rams. The other, quoted by *Rashi* (*Shabbos* 81b) talks of people using plants. This explanation assumes these were not two independent customs. Rather it was one common custom that varied according to means. People on the upper end of the financial scale could afford more. Those on the lower end did less.

these practices. Because of their objections, we will see that parts of the *minhag* have been cut out, leaving behind just the basics.

For Who and By Who

Who traditionally had *kaparos* performed for them? This depended on the era and area. Some communities performed it for all children,[68] some just for boys,[69] some for all members of the household,[70] and some only for the patriarch.

We have described the common practice—which still continues today—of people reading the *pesukim* and revolving the *kaparah*-chicken around their heads themselves. Other early sources describe the *rav* or *tzaddik* reading the verses for the penitent. As he read, he would either place one hand on the head of the animal and the other on the head of the penitent, or encircle the penitent's head with the animal[71] showing that any punishment due the person should now befall the animal. Having a third party perform the ceremony was based on the *korban* precedent: The *Avodah* of a *korban* was performed by the *Kohen* on behalf of the owner. Similarly, the *kaparos* ceremony was carried out by someone other than the penitent.

In some communities, it was the *shaliach tzibbur* or the *shochet* who performed the ceremony. It is possible that the reason for this was that the *shaliach tzibbur* often acted

---

68   See *Rashi Shabbos* 81 v. s. *Hai*.

69   Opinion of the Mechaber, *Orach Chaim* §605.

70   This is the most popular *minhag* addressed in the *sefarim*.

71   Placing one hand on the animal and one on the penitent, or encircling the penitents head with the bird, may have developed to replace *semichah*. See previous page.

as the *shaliach Beis Din*. In the time of the *Rishonim*, people would subject themselves to the punishments of *Beis Din* on Erev Yom Kippur. They would come before the *shaliach tzibbur*, who represented *Beis Din*, to receive *malkos*, the thirty-nine lashes administered for lesser infractions.[72] He would then mete out, on the chicken, capital punishment,[73] the punishment *Beis Din* imposed for major transgressions.[74]

Pesukim and Rotations

In many communities, the *kaparos* ceremony began with the recitation of *pesukim*. Other communities said the *pesukim* after the chicken was revolved around the head, while yet others said them between the *berachah* and the *shechitah*.[75]

The *pesukim* (which will be explored in depth later[76]) are selections from *Tehillim*[77] and *Iyov*.[78] Most communities said the same *pesukim* we say today. Some *sefarim* record a *minhag* to say more *pesukim*, while others said less. The *pesukim*, which deal with *teshuvah*, man's obligation to acknowledge Hashem and give thanks to Him, redemption and salvation, were added to help people focus on *teshuvah* and to ensure that their actions did not appear to be sorcery.[79]

---

72   *Maharil, Erev Yom Kippur 5.*
73   See below page 51, section "*Arba Misos.*"
74   Heard from Rabbi Yaakov Baruch Gestner.
75   *Tashbetz (Koton)* 125 quoted in *Bach* §605:2.
76   Chap. 13.
77   *Tehillim* 107.
78   *Iyov* 33.
79   *Meiri, Chibur HaTeshuvah*, 2:8, page 398.

After reciting the introductory verses, the penitent would rotate the animal around his head and say, "This is my exchange, this is my replacement, this is my atonement. This animal will go to its death, and I will be preserved for a good and long life." Since the head is the most significant part of the body and often used to allegorically represent the entire body, circling the animal around the head showed that if a bad decree were due to befall this man, it should transfer to the animal.

My *rebbe*, HaGaon Reb Dovid Feinstein, *shlita*, suggested that rotating the bird around the head may have been a converse form of *semichah*. Because people wanted to do some form of *semichah* without the appearance of a *korban* ritual, they rotated the animal around their heads instead of putting their hands on the animal's head.

The verses were repeated several times and the animal revolved around the head three, seven, or nine times.

The rationale of repeating the ceremony three times is in line with many other items that are repeated thrice for emphasis. For example, all rabbinic pronouncements, like *hataras nedarim*[80] and *Beis Din's* pronouncement of *kiddush ha-chodesh*,[81] are said three times. Repeating something three times reinforces the point being made.[82] Here, too, the three revolutions strengthen the relationship between the person and the bird.

The number seven is also easy to understand. In the Torah, seven is often associated with holiness: seven days in a week, seven years in a *shemitah* cycle, etc. Furthermore, we find the number seven used in particular with regard to circuits: seven circuits

---

80   *Yoreh De'ah* §228:3; see also Shach 6.
81   See *Rosh Hashanah* 24a, the pronouncement of "*mekudash*" was said a total of three times, once by the *Av Beis Din* and twice by the attendees.
82   In our daily lives too, people repeat words like "no" three times for emphasis.

around the *mizbe'ach* on *Succos*[83] and seven circuits around Yericho.[84] Seven is also an important number in the purification process. The *metzorah*[85] is *tamei* and must endure a lengthy and involved process to become *tahor*. The number seven plays a significant role in his purification process.[86]

There is a very interesting statement in the Gemara apropos to circling overhead, the number seven, and transferring. The Gemara[87] discusses a cure in which the afflicted waves a mug of water over his head seven times. After saying his incantation, he throws the cup of water into the river. In the instance of the Gemara, the afflicted is trying to transfer an illness from himself to the river. Similarly, during *kaparos* the sinner attempts to "remove his sins" from himself to somewhere else.

It is not so clear why it is done nine times. However, this seems to be the most prevalent custom. When saying "*zeh chalifasi,*" many people rotate the chicken three times—once at *chalifasi,* then at *temurasi* and finally at *kaparasi.* They then repeat the phrase three times, for a total of nine rotations. It would thus appear that the nine times are really "three times three."

זה חליפתי, זה תמורתי, זה כפרתי. זה התרנגול ילך למיתה, ואני אכנס לחיים טובים וארוכים ולשלום.

"THIS IS MY EXCHANGE, THIS IS MY REPLACEMENT, THIS IS MY ATONEMENT. THIS CHICKEN WILL GO TO ITS DEATH, AND I WILL EMBARK ON A GOOD LIFE, OF LONGEVITY AND PEACE."

---

83   *Succah* 43b, 45a.

84   *Yehoshua* 6:3 *et al.*

85   *Metzorah*—someone suffering from an illness similar to leprosy.

86   *Negaim* 14:10.

87   *Shabbos* 66b וליהדר שב זימני על רישיה, (ויקיפנו סביבות ראשו - רש״י).

Exchange, Replace, Atone

The wording of the principal phrase (see box on previous page) said during the *kaparos* ceremony was chosen carefully. The key words, "exchange," "replacement," and "atonement," were chosen from among the possible synonyms and arranged for the acronym they form. The first letters of the Hebrew for "exchange" (חלפתי), "replacement" (תמורתי), and "atonement" (כפרתי) form the acronym "חתך" (*Chosech*)—the name of the *malach* of life.[88]

The use of the word *temurah* (replacement) has unfavorable connotations in relation to *korbanos*, and has therefore been challenged.[89] The problem lies in the *halachic* meaning of the word. In halachah, the term represents the illegal transfer of sanctity from a *korban* to a non-*korban* animal. The result of a *temurah* is that *both* animals become sanctified.

Although *kaparos* does not involve an animal *korban*, the *Acharonim* found the mimicking of an activity that the Torah forbids—or even just the use of a word that represents a concept forbidden by the Torah—distasteful. They further objected to the analogy itself: If through real *temurah* of the *korbanos*, both animals are sanctified, then if we use the word *temurah* in connection to *kaparos*, both the person and the chicken are to share a common fate—the exact opposite of the intention of the custom![90]

Despite the above concerns, the use of the word *temurah* has endured. In using the term, we are not referring to *korbanos* and not alluding to any kind of transfer of sanctity. Obviously, there isn't any "real" *korban* here. Nevertheless, there are those who still

---

88   *M.B.* § 605:3.

89   *Shu"t Be'er Sheva* 53.

90   *Aruch HaShulchan* §605:4.

recommend that we change *temurasi* to *tachti*.[91] Although they are synonyms, the latter word has no connotation involving *korbanos*. This change has not caught on.

Semichah **and** *Arba Misos Beis Din*

After reciting the verses, the penitent used to place his hands on the head of the bird or animal and recite *viduy*, as though it were a *korban*—a process known as *semichah*. Then, in keeping with the rule of *korbanos*—תיכף לסמיכה שחיטה, meaning the *shechitah* must immediately follow the *semichah*—the *kaparah* was slaughtered immediately. Over time, though, the practice of *semichah* was seen as making *kaparos* too similar to *korbanos*, and *semichah* was discontinued.[92]

Some *Acharonim* defended the custom, saying that this *semichah* was not the same as the *semichah* of *korbanos*. Rather, it is related to a different type of *semichah* called *semichas zekainim*—appointment as an elder. During the ceremony of *semichas zekainim* the elders symbolically placed their hands on the head of a disciple to pass the mantle of leadership to him. *Kaparos* is supposed to accomplish something similar. By placing our hands on the head of the animal before *shechitah,* we transfer all the harm and penalties due us to the animal.[93]

There is a *minhag* to subject the animal to the four *misos* of *Beis Din*. This is in line with the themes of being aroused to *teshuvah* through the death of the animal and of the animal replacing the person. As he watched the punishments being administered to the animal, the person was expected to review his own actions. If he discovered something

---

91   See *Aruch HaShulchan* §605:4.

92   *Taz* §605:3. See also *Mishnah Berurah* 8.

93   *Siddur Rav Yacov Emden* (*Ya'avetz*).

that could have resulted in his deserving capital punishment, watching the animal die was a powerful incentive to *teshuvah*. And if he had deserved punishment before doing *teshuvah*, the animal's death would now take the place of his.

The four primary punishments of *Beis Din* were: *sekilah*—stoning, *sereifah*—burning, *hereg*—death by sword, and *chenek*—strangulation.

With the exception of *sekilah*, these four forms of corporal punishment were carried out during or after *shechitah*. For *sekilah*, the chicken was thrown to the ground or its head was stepped on prior to *shechitah*. *Sereifah*, burning, was accomplished when the feathers were singed before *kashering* or when it was heated to be cooked. *Chenek*, strangulation, was done when the *shochet* pulled the skin of the neck tight before *shechting*, and *hereg*, death by sword, was carried out with the *shochet's* knife.

The *poskim* were worried about the potential harm that could happen to the chicken if it were thrown or stepped on before *shechitah*, which might render it a *tereifah*—unfit for eating. They therefore encouraged the people to do so only after *shechitah*.[94] I once watched an elderly person step on the head of his live chicken and break its neck. When the *shochet* rightfully refused to *shecht* it, the man put up a fuss and eventually left in a huff.

When to Perform the *Minhag*

The timing of *kaparos* varied from place to place.

---

94   *Shar Hatziyun* (Mishnah Berurah) §605:2. See also *Elef Hamagen* §605:13.

The inaugural festivities of the Beis HaMikdash—the center of atonement for all sins—began on the eighth day of Tishrei. For this reason, some had the custom to choose their chicken—their *kaparah*—on this day.[95]

There had been a custom to perform *kaparos* on Erev Rosh Hashanah. This was based on the Talmudic axiom, "תכלה שנה וקלליותיה—May the year and its sorrows end."[96] This maxim accentuates our hope that the penalties accrued this year will not carry over into the next. In this context, it is our wish that our sorrows end with the close of the current year. We hope there is no continuation into the new year. *Kaparos* expresses a similar concept. In case there was an outstanding decree against the person, the chicken's death should absolve the person, and prevent a carryover of the decree into the following year.

As explained in the first chapter, *kaparos* also serves as an omen that the coming year be filled with Hashem's kindness and compassion. Like the *simanim* eaten on the night of Rosh Hashanah, which set a positive tone for the coming year, *kaparos* symbolizes our hope that the future year be one of forgiveness.

The majority of the initiating *simanim* are performed on Rosh Hashanah. Ideally this *siman* too should have been planned for Rosh Hashanah itself. Why was it done earlier?

A similar question can be asked regarding the idea of *Akeidah* discussed in the third chapter. Rosh Hashanah is the anniversary of the *Akeidah* and many of the Rosh Hashanah *minhagim* are designed to call attention to it. For example, the Satan tried to prevent Avraham from going to the *Akeidah*. In one foiled ploy, he attempted to block

---

95   *Siddur Rav Yacov Emden (Ya'avetz).*
96   *Megillah* 31b.

Avraham's passage with a raging river. Avraham forged right on. To commemorate Avraham's dedication, there is a custom to visit a river on Rosh Hashanah day.[97]

Later, during the *Akeidah,* a ram appeared to Avraham Avinu. The ram's horns were tangled in the brush. Avraham offered the ram on the *mizbe'ach* instead of his son. The head of a ram eaten on Rosh Hashanah eve[98] and the ram's horn *shofar*[99] blown Rosh Hashanah morning recall this event.

For both of these reasons—the augury of the *simanim* and to commemorate the *Akeidah*—the best time to do *kaparos*, theoretically, would have been on Rosh Hashanah itself. Why was this *minhag* advanced to Erev Rosh Hashanah?

There are two issues with doing *kaparos* on Rosh Hashanah. First, it is not permissible to *shecht* unnecessarily on Yom Tov.[100] Second, animals are *muktzah* on Yom Tov and handling them is forbidden.[101] Therefore, the *kaparos* ceremony was moved up a day to Erev Rosh Hashanah in some communities, or to the following week,[102] as in our communities.

---

97   *Mishnah Berurah* §583:8.

98   *O. C.* §583:2.

99   *Mishnah Berurah* §586:2.

100   The general rule is any food preparation that could not have been done before Yom Tov may be done on Yom Tov. Preparatory activity that could have been done before Yom Tov may not be done on Yom Tov (*Orach Chaim* §495:1). *Mishnah Berurah* (8) lists meat as a food that spoils over time and therefore may be *shechted* on Yom Tov. He is referring to meat *shechted* on Erev Yom Tov and left unrefrigerated for an extended period, overnight or longer. However, since meat *shechted* just before Yom Tov would stay fresh until the holiday, and in fact that would be the usual time to *shecht* the meat for the evening *seudah*, one may not *shecht* on the first night of a Yom Tov.
        See also *Shu't Yehuda Yaleh (Mahari Asad)* 164, where he records a *minhag* not to *shecht* on Rosh Hashanah since it is a time to exhibit heightened compassion.

101   *O.C.* 497–498.

102   See *Otzar HaTefillos, Tikun Tefillah* toward the end.

Zeh Kaporosi

Performing *kaparos* earlier, on Erev Rosh Hashanah, offered the benefit of having the *simanim* in place before the onset of the new year.

The rationale for delaying it for the following week is that the entire *aseres yemei teshuvah* are still considered the beginning of the year. They also have a strong connection to the *Akeidah*. Every morning of these ten days we invoke the *Akeidah* during the *selichos*.

These reasons for postponing the ceremony until after Rosh Hashanah are in addition to the other reasons cited below.

As mentioned, the most widespread *minhag* was to perform *kaparos* on Erev Yom Kippur. Originally, the *minhag* was to do it during the day.[103] The Arizal, based on *Kabbalah*, taught that is was best done just before daybreak.[104]

Until recent times it was customary for the *shochet* to call on the families that required his services. It was not possible for him to visit all that many families in the moments before daybreak of Erev Yom Kippur, so he began his rounds in the beginning of the night.

In the period of the middle *Acharonim*,[105] some of the *Rabbanim* started to worry that the *shochtim* would become weary from trudging around all night. Going from family to family to *shecht*, the *shochet* would become too tired to *shecht* carefully.

Many *Acharonim*[106] offered suggestions to solve the problem. The ideas ranged from counseling the *shochtim* on the importance of focused/undistracted *shechitah*, to restricting the

---

103   In many *Rishonim* this custom, along with *malkos* and *tevilah*, etc., are listed among the customs for the day of Erev Yom Kippur.

104   *Mishnah Berurah* §605:2.

105   It seems the first to mention the problem was the *Simlah Chadashah* (§18:12), printed in 5493 (1733).

106   See *Simlah Chadashah* §18:12; *Kreisei U'pelesei, Kreisei* §18:17; *Pri Megadim* §605:1; *Chayei Adam* 143:4; *Mishnah Berurah* §605:2; *Kaf Hachaim* §605:11–13 and others.

shochtim to central, supervised locations, using money instead of chickens[107] or encouraging people to do *kaparos* earlier in the week. Most of these suggestions have been implemented today.

Kaparos and the subsequent *shechitah* were to be done on Erev Yom Kippur. There is a discussion, rooted in *Kabbalah,* as to when is the preferred time to *shecht.* The choices are the night before Yom Kippur,[108] the day of Erev Yom Kippur,[109] or between pre-dawn *selichos* and *Shacharis.*[110] The contemporary communities that are particular to do *kaparos* on Erev Yom Kippur have their established *minhagim* as to when to *shecht.*

Discarding the Innards

The original *minhag* was to cast away the innards of the bird or animal after *shechitah.* As a matter of fact, two of the inferences in the Gemara concerning *kaparos* are about throwing away the animal's viscera[111] on Erev Yom Kippur. The Gemara tells of Rami bar Tamri, who came to a town on Erev Yom Kippur. He found many livers

---

107   The first (and only) mention of using money for *kaparos* was as a solution to this concern. This topic will be covered in full in chap. 9, see page 77.

108   This was the most prevalent practice, as cited in all the *Acharonim.* Most likely it was to satisfy the *kabbalistic* requirement that the *shechitah* happen before dawn.

109   This was the practice mentioned in the *Rishonim.* The *Elyah Rabbah* writes that this is also the proper time according to *Kabbalah.*

110   Arizal, quoted in *Mishnah Berurah* §605:2.

111   Viscera—collectively the internal organs [of an animal], especially those in the abdominal cavity.

and kidneys[112] that had been taken and then discarded by the ravens. The *mefarshim* explain that the local *Yidden* had slaughtered their *kaparos*-animals and discarded their innards in accordance with the *minhag*. Their reasoning is as follows: It is unlikely that the ravens could have, on their own, collected so many livers and kidneys from inside homes. It must therefore be assumed that the livers and kidneys were intentionally thrown into the streets for the birds. The birds collected the organs, and because of the abundance, they could not eat them all, so they abandoned some.

Four[113] reasons are given for the custom of discarding the innards:

1. We wish to show sympathy toward the birds that have a difficult time collecting their food. We hope that Hashem will look kindly upon our sympathetic gesture and, in turn, provide our sustenance with ease.[114]

2. In case it was decreed that our bodies be harmed, the decree should be fulfilled with the destruction of the animal's entrails.[115]

3. The organs of a *korban* were placed on the *mizbe'ach* and not eaten by the one bringing it. In a similar way, the innards of the *kaparah* are not to be eaten by the one who benefited from the ceremony.

---

112   This is how the Rosh (*Yoma* §8:23) and Tur (605) and many *Rishonim* quote the Gemara. According to our version of the Gemara, this is a fusion of two incidents, both of which occurred on Erev Yom Kippur. In one, (*Chullin* 95b) an *Amora*, Rav Nachman of Nahardaah, happened upon livers and kidneys discarded by the ravens. In the other (*Chullin* 110a), Rami bar Tamri found an udder discarded by the local people. The *Rishonim*, however, combine both stories. Some suggest that these *Rishonim* understood both Gemaras to be discussing *kaparos*.

113   The first three reasons apply equally to both animals and birds. The fourth applies only to birds.

114   *Mishnah Berurah* §605:9.

115   *Siddur Hagra*—*Ishei Yisroel* (Berman).

4. The fourth and most widely known reason applies specifically to birds: Since birds feed in the fields of others, they constantly consume stolen property. To show our disdain for theft, we discard the crop,[116] full of its stolen goods, along with the organs that absorb the stolen food first. With this act, we try to inspire ourselves to stay far away from theft,[117] and we hope that Hashem will look favorably upon our efforts and forgive us for our injustices.[118]

The idea of casting aside these organs has a precedent in the *olas ha'oaf*, the burnt-bird *korban*. Typically, the entire *olah* with all of its internal organs was burned on the *mizbe'ach*. However, with the burnt-bird offering, although the bird was small to begin with, the entire digestive tract was removed and discarded. The *Medrash*[119] explains that since the bird swallows food belonging to others, Hashem does not allow the swallowing organs on His *mizbe'ach*.

Nowadays, with modern sanitation requirements, we can no longer cast the viscera to the birds and are unable to fulfill this part of the original *minhag*. We still dispose of the organs in fulfillment of the other reasons.

Plants and Chickens

Most communities and people always used birds or animals for *kaparos*, though there was, as mentioned previously, the custom cited by Rashi to use plants:

---

116   Crop—sac in the neck of the chicken (and most kosher birds) that holds the food until it is ingested.
117   Although technically this type of feeding is not theft, since this is the natural order of the world, on this holy day we wish to distance ourselves even from things remotely related to theft.
118   *Mishnah Berurah* §605:9.
119   *Vayikra Rabbah* 3:4, cited by Rashi, *Vayikra* 1:16.

Twenty-two or fifteen days before Rosh Hashanah, palm-branch baskets filled with soil and animal manure were prepared for every boy and girl in the household. Bean seeds were planted in them. This was called *parfisa*. On Erev Rosh Hashanah, every [child] took his potted plant and rotated it over his head seven times, chanting, "This substitutes for this, this is my replacement, this is my exchange," and then cast [the pot] into the river. [120]

The idea of using a plant to represent a person is based on the verse, "For man is [like] a tree [in] the field."[121] It is also a play on words. The Hebrew word *zera* means both *plant* and *offspring*.[122] If harm was supposed to befall the child, let it pass to the plant instead.[123] After passing the plant over the child's head seven times the plant was tossed into the river.

The intention was to prevent illnesses in general, with a special emphasis on *asscera*. *Asscera*, a particularly painful childhood disease, caused swelling in the throat and eventual death through suffocation. The children—*zera*—who were vulnerable to *asscera*,[124] hoped that through their plant—also called *zera*—they could discharge any harmful decrees against themselves. They would associate the plant with themselves by circling it over their heads. Since the Gemara[125] equates the suffering of *asscera* to the pain of drowning, they would then toss the plant into the river allowing the plant to "suffer" for them.[126]

---

120   *Rashi* to *Shabbos* 81b s.v. *Hai Parfisa*.

121   *Devarim* 20:19.

122   *Siddur Rav Yacov Emden* (*Ya'avetz*).

123   *Chasam Sofer, Shabbos* 81b, s.v. *Haminhag*.

124   See *Tanis* 27b, תנו רבנן אנשי משמר וכו', ברביעי - על אסכרא שלא תיפול על התינוקות. There is also a special *selichah*, א-ל נא רפא נא תחלואי גפן פוריה, recited at the beginning and end of the winter (בה"ב) to protect children from this horrible death.

125   *Kesubos* 30b, ומי שנתחייב חנק - או טובע בנהר או מת בסרונכי (אסכרה - רש"י).

126   *Chasam Sofer Shabbos* 81b, s.v. *Haminhag*.

According to this *minhag*, *kaparos* was done only for children.

Since this *minhag* is not mentioned in any other source, it would seem that it was never widespread.[127] It is doubtful if even Rashi himself ever used plants. Both of his famous *talmidim*, *Machzor Vitri* and *Sefer HaOrah*, specify to use chickens. Moreover, Rashi's words, "I have *found* in the *Teshuvas HaGeonim*," imply that this custom was not familiar to people even in his times.

At one point, the chicken became the popular animal for *kaparos*, perhaps because unlike sheep and cows, it is not acceptable for use as a *korban*. The use of chickens made it very clear that the *kaparos* were *not korbanos*.

Other possibilities for the popularity of chickens are because most people owned them, or they were affordable,[128] or they are small and easy to wave around the head. Some suggest that chickens were chosen because, as mentioned earlier, they are called *gever*, which is also a term for man.[129] The jarring similarities in names may help jolt the person to *teshuvah*. *Gever* also represents the *kabbalistic* concept of *gevurah*, a theme central to *kaparos*.[130]

Some *Rishonim* advocated using white chickens for *kaparos*, since white is the color of purity and forgiveness. Thus, the color both represented forgiveness and encouraged

---

127   I have not found any other source that says there is a *minhag* to use a potted plant. As I will point out at the end of chap. 7, while not an active *minhag*, potted plants are listed as an option for someone who does not have access to a chicken.

       However, doing so is no simple matter. To implement the custom described in the *Teshuvos HaGeonim* you would need an edible, potted plant. These are not readily available. Even in the *teshuvah* quoted, the children had to especially prepare the plants. (See *Orchos Rabbenu*, vol. 2, *Yom Kippur* 6.)

128   *Tur* §605.

129   *Gever* means both man (male, e.g., לֹא יִהְיֶה כְלִי גֶבֶר עַל אִשָּׁה [דברים כב:ה]) and mankind (e.g., מַה יִּתְאוֹנֵן אָדָם חָי גֶּבֶר עַל חֲטָאָיו [איכה ג:לט]). In this context it connotes mankind.

130   See *Kaf Hachaim O.C.* §605:5 for an explanation of this theme.

the participant to repent. Others,[131] as we will see below, were opposed to the use of a white chicken. Although it is recorded that the Maharil appreciated a white chicken, he probably did not especially seek one.[132]

The familiar white chicken, so common today, is a relatively new innovation, appearing within the last forty years. Before then, a white chicken was an albino—a mutation—and was rare. For reasons of their own, idol worshipers preferred these chickens and would seek them out, paying a premium for them. The Gemara thus calls the intentional selection of a white chicken *darkei ha'emori*—*avodah zarah*-style—and forbids the practice.[133] The question at the center of the debate as it relates to *kaparos* was whether a person's legitimate intention to use white to signify *kaparah* counterbalances the problem of *darkei ha'emori*.

The *Acharonim* advocated using white birds when available, provided they were not specifically sought after. However, they were rare and inaccessible most of the time.

The issue is not relevant today. Since the industry automatically supplies white chickens it is not considered as though the individual is specifically selecting white chickens. In addition, since nowadays white chickens are readily available, people would not view selecting a white chicken as practicing idolatry. It follows that it would not be forbidden because of *darkei ha'emori*.[134]

---

131   *Bach* §605:2.

132   *Taz* §605:2.

133   *Avodah Zarah* 13b, *et al*.

134   See *Machatzis HaShekel* to *Magen Avraham* §605:3.

CHAPTER FIVE

TAKING YOUR BIRDS HOME ALIVE:
CARING FOR YOUR BIRDS AND AVOIDING *TZA'AR BA'ALEI CHAIM*

Some people like to take live chickens home. They wish to focus on the ritual without all the commotion inherent in a *kaparos* center. Or, bringing the chicken home is done as a convenience for an overworked housewife, young children, or the elderly by allowing them to participate without leaving home.

If you take the birds home, there are several *halachos* that apply while they are under your care.

It is forbidden to eat before feeding animals that are dependent on you for their food. Even snacking is prohibited, although drinking is permitted.[135] Therefore, if the chickens are kept for a while or overnight, they must be fed and watered.

Chickens must be fed twice a day and need water regularly. If you will be keeping them for only a short while, (e.g., 2–3 hours in the middle of the day), you do not need to feed them and may eat without restrictions because we can assume they were fed at the *kaparos* center and it is not the time for their next feeding.

If one person is designated to care for the animals, the rules apply only to him. Other family members may eat before the animals are fed.

Zeh Kaporosi

---

135   *Mishnah Berurah* §167:40.

Feeding chickens in a crowded box can be tricky.[136] Frequently, the chickens will refuse to eat while jammed in a box. It is often hard to find a suitable water container that will not spill, which creates a mess and leaves no water for the birds. Letting the chickens out of the box presents its own difficulties, such as a runaway.

These common problems affect most people who have animals for only a short term. There are no easy solutions to any of these problems. Therefore, try to return your chickens to the market as soon as possible.

The Commercial Situation

These are the basic *halachos* of animal care. In theory, these rules apply everywhere. However, in practice, at commercial plants the story is quite different. Whether right or wrong, poultry processors in the United States have their own way of doing things.

Based on recommendations of the Health Department, it is the practice of all commercial poultry processors not to feed the birds for twenty-four hours before slaughter. Less food in the chicken translates into less waste to be removed from the chicken. This means that the consumer gets a cleaner and more sanitary meal.

The chickens do not benefit from last-minute feedings. When a chicken, like all birds, swallows food, it does not go directly to the stomach. Instead, the food is held in a special pouch in the throat called a crop. As the bird requires nourishment, it brings the food down

---

136   Although the vast majority of the world's chickens spend their entire life in a crowded cage, adequate measures are in place to allow the birds to eat. The concern here is of chickens crowded into an unfamiliar, dark, poorly ventilated box. The birds will be uneasy and lose interest in their food.

to its stomach (gizzard) to be ground and digested. Typically, food can stay in the crop for a day or longer. In commercially produced birds, there is frequently a small amount of food left in their crops, despite the fact that they have not been fed in several hours.

(Local live markets like to stuff the birds as much as they can before selling them. They sell the live birds by the pound and an extra pound of corn adds considerably to the price of the meat!)

Feeding the birds just prior to the *shechitah* raises additional points that must be dealt with. Food in the swallowing tract[137] can impair the *shechitah*. If, during *shechitah*, the knife strikes stiff or hard food, the *shechitah* is invalid.[138] Besides, any food that comes in contact with the knife can dull the blade.

The *shochet* will also need to contend with the mess caused by food in the swallowing tract. Oftentimes during *shechitah*, the swallowing tract is fully opened. Anything in the esophagus, from the mouth through the crop, is liable to spill out. This brings us back to our original concerns of mess, stench, and sanitation.[139]

This being the case, it is rare that any grower will feed his poultry before sending them for processing.

Whatever happens at the poultry processors aside, if you take birds home, you must abide by the *halachos*.

THE *PUPIK* (GIZZARD) WITH THE PROVENTRICULUS STILL ATTACHED

---

137   The swallowing tract of birds extends from the mouth until the stomach. It includes all the tubes and organs along the way that carry the food down to the gizzard (stomach). These include, mouth, esophagus, crop, proventriculus, etc.
During *shechitah* the esophagus is supposed to be cut fully open. (See *Yoreh De'ah* §21:1, §25:1)

138   *Yoreh De'ah* §23:2.

139   The last two paragraphs were inspired by *Kuntres V'yevareich Kol Bassar* by Rav Amitai BenDavid (author of *Sichas Chullin*).

CHAPTER SIX

Choosing Your Chickens:
The type and number of chickens to use

A man should ideally take a rooster—an adult male chicken that can crow[140]—and a woman should take a hen . However, it is impractical to provide crowing roosters on such a large scale. There probably aren't enough in the entire United States to service the *kaparos* industry. Besides, their tough flesh is not very useful once they are *shechted*.

> In pre-war Europe, those who could afford it were careful to use white chickens; roosters for men and hens for women. Those who could not afford it were happy if they had a chicken.

Therefore, the *kaparos* industry uses young chickens between four and six weeks old. At this age, all the experts agree that it is impossible to tell a male from a female. It is possible that the chickens were segregated at day one, the only time before maturity that you can tell the difference. However, since there is no reason for commercial producers to separate the males from

---

140   The term *gever* refers to a chicken with the ability to crow. See Gemara *Yoma* 20b and 21a. *Mekor Chaim* §605:1.

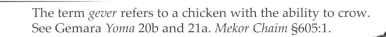

WHITE KAPAROS HEN

the females, it is more likely that the chickens are a mixed lot. (Contrary to popular belief, these chickens are not raised for *kaparos*.) So we accept the selections of the *kaparos* workers[141] and hope they are right.[142]

The Maharil writes, "A pregnant woman should take two chickens, one being for the baby."[143] It is unclear why he required an expectant mother to use two chickens. It would seem reasonable that he felt that since two people can share one *kaparah*, one chicken covered the mother and possible daughter. The second chicken is a male in case the child is a boy.[144] (This is the consensus of most *Acharonim*.)

Alternatively, it might be because two people cannot share the same chicken. One is for the mother and the second for the child, the gender being unimportant.[145]

Many *Acharonim* felt it was unnecessary to use a separate hen for an unborn daughter. Analogous to *korbanos*, where two people can share one *korban*,[146] two people may join to use one chicken for *kaparos*. Therefore, a mother and her unborn daughter do not need

---

141   Theoretically, if the chickens all hatched the same day and consumed equal amounts of food, the males would be slightly larger, with taller and darker combs—if you are capable of discerning such subtle differences.

142   Many *Rishonim* instruct men to use roosters and women hens. However, not all *Rishonim* mention this detail. In fact, the language of some *Rishonim* sounds like both genders can use any type of chicken. See *Mordechai, Yoma* 723. The Arizal, cited below, required the gender to match even for an unborn child. However, *Eishel Avraham* (*But'chetch*) §605 allows an error in gender for anyone, even according to the Arizal. See also footnote 145.

143   *Minhagim*; Yom Kippur §3, quoted by the Rama §605. The text here follows the interpretation of the *Magen Avraham* §605:2. Others explain the Rama to mean, two chickens are to be used for the baby aside from what she takes for herself. (See *Mekor Chaim*.)

144   See *Magen Avraham* §605:2.

145   I found this idea in *Hilchos Chag B'Chag* (Rav M.M. Karp, p. רע"ז, §22). I included it as background for the *Pri Megadim* quoted in footnote 149. If this explanation is true, it can also justify the modern practice of using a mixed lot of chickens.

146   Two individuals may at times share the expense and bring a joint *korban nedavah*—voluntary gift offering.

more than one *kaparah*. (A son, being of a different gender, may still need a separate bird.) Moreover, since the halachah follows the Talmudic opinion that the fetus is part of the mother,[147] the mother's *kaparah* can cover any unborn child, even a son.

This discussion assumes *kaparos* is related to a *korban*. However, other *Acharonim* offer a different reason to do *kaparos* for an unborn child. As we said, the death of the animal distracts the Satan so that he should not harm the person. Accordingly, each individual, even an unborn child, would need his or her own chicken decoy.

The Arizal required a pregnant woman to use three chickens. He was of the opinion that every individual needs his or her own *kaparah*, and that the gender must match.[148]

The instructions in the *machzorim* tell the pregnant woman to hold both chickens at once and recite the formula in plural, "These are our," etc. It would be a very neat feat if pregnant women were able to execute that!

The contemporary *minhag* seems to be that the woman (or her husband) takes a hen and recites, "This is our…" and then a rooster and says, "This is your…"

Many women, not wishing to announce their status to the public, do not take additional chickens in the early months of pregnancy.[149]

---

147   **עובר ירך אמו**—*Temurah* 25a.

148   *Be'er Heitiv* §605:2.

149   I heard from my *rebbe*, HaGaon Rav Dovid Feinstein, *shlita*, that every pregnant woman may rely on the *Pri Megadim* (605:2) who allows the mother and fetus to share one chicken. He added that this had, in fact, been the common practice of the poor.

CHAPTER SEVEN

SHLUG KAPAROS!

Instructions You Won't Find in the Machzor

Now that we have decided on the number of birds and their types, we have to learn how to use them. You want to be able to hold the chicken in a way that it cannot escape or harm you. At the same time you want to hold it in a way that you can focus on *teshuvah* and saying the *pesukim* without distraction.

The truth is that holding a chicken in one's bare hands is the part that makes some people squeamish. This is a turn-off point for some people. It need not be that way. Chickens are very compliant animals. If you treat them fairly, they will oblige you. With a little forethought and consideration anybody can hold a chicken properly and with ease.

The goal is to hold the chicken in a way that is both comfortable for you and the chicken, while allowing you full control of the bird.

> **TO HOLD LEFT-HANDED: PLACE THE RIGHT WING OVER THE LEFT. PUT YOUR LEFT HAND UNDER THE BASE OF THE WINGS AND CLOSE YOUR THUMB AND FINGER AROUND THE WINGS. DO NOT SQUEEZE.**

You will need to cross the wings and flip it over so that the head points to the ground.

To hold right-handed:

- Place the left wing over the right.

LIFT THE WINGS.

DRAW THEM TOGETHER

- Put your right hand under the base of the wings and close your thumb and finger around the wings. Do not squeeze.

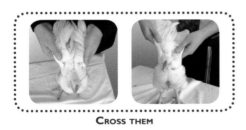
CROSS THEM

GRIP THEM

- Flip the chicken over so that the wings point to the ground and the body rests on the back of your hand.

- If it makes you feel more secure, you may hold the feet with your other hand.

LIFT THE CHICKEN

The chicken should cooperate when held firmly and calmly like as described; just don't jerk it.
TIP: Handle your bird gently and it will remain calm.

Move away from the crowds, commotion and smell, in order to say the *pesukim*. When saying "*zeh chalifasi*," wave the chicken around your head according to your *minhag*.[150] After the rite, you should immediately present the chicken to the *shochet* for *shechitah*.

SHLOG KAPAROS!

Observe the *shechitah*.

After *shechitah*, do *kisuy hadam*. (See section on *kisuy hadam*.)

UNFORTUNATELY, THESE CHICKENS ARE BEING ALLOWED TO WATCH THE SHECHITAH. IT WOULD BE BETTER IF THEY WERE HELD IN A WAY THAT THEY COULD NOT SEE THE SHECHITAH.

Preferably, one animal should not watch the slaughter of another. Therefore, when standing in queue for the shochet, try to position the chickens so that they cannot watch the *shechitah*.[151]

You First

If you are planning to perform the ceremony for family members, it is preferable to do it for yourself first. This is

---

150   There are different *minhagim* as to when and how many times to rotate the bird over your head. Consult your *machzor* or your parents to determine your *minhag*.

151   See *Yoreh De'ah* §36:14 and *Yad Ephraim* there.

modeled after the *Kohen Gadol* on Yom Kippur, who first brought his own *korbanos* and then the *korbanos* for the rest of Klal Yisrael.[152] As in the original *minhag* where the *tzaddik* did the ceremony for the others, you must first do your own *teshuvah*, and then help others in their quest for penitence.

Shechitah

Shechitah, slaughtering the animal in the presence of the penitent, has always been an essential part of *kaparos*. Possibly it is the most important part.[153]

Today, unfortunately, immediate *shechitah* is no longer the universal practice because it is too difficult to maintain. One problem is, since many *kaparos*-centers are in makeshift setups, they do not have the space or equipment to process the *shechted* birds. Besides, it is unusual for a center to have the facilities necessary to store so many processed chickens. In addition, many centers don't want the mess associated with *shechting* and eviscerating[154] the birds. In the United States and elsewhere, there are also concerns relating to the Health Department

STEP BY STEP SUMMARY

LIFT BOTH OF THE CHICKEN'S WINGS. EXTEND THEM FULLY. DRAW THEM TOGETHER. CROSS THE WINGS. PLACE LEFT OVER RIGHT FOR A RIGHT-HANDED GRIP. PUT YOUR RIGHT HAND BENEATH THE WINGS AND CLOSE YOUR FINGERS OVER THE WINGS AS SHOWN. GENTLY FLIP THE BIRD ONTO ITS BACK. (THE CHICKEN'S BODY WILL NOW BE RESTING ON THE BACK OF YOUR HAND.) ROTATE OVERHEAD AS YOU SAY "ZEH CHALIFASI."

---

152   *Shevuos* 14a.

153   See page 44, section, "Symbolizing a *Korban*."

154   Eviscerate—remove the internal organs (innards) from the abdomen of an animal carcass.

and the ever-watchful eyes of our enemies.[155] Many centers cannot afford to keep a *shochet* on hand during the slower afternoon sessions. This is a pity, because without *shechitah* the ceremony is incomplete.

Chicken Alternatives

Not everybody has access to chickens. A person who cannot obtain a chicken may use (in this order): a) a kosher bird or animal that is not acceptable for a *korban*, b) a fish, c) a potted plant[156] (discard the plant after use), d) money equivalent to the value of a chicken,[157] e) any amount[158] of money.[159]

When using an item other than a chicken, the formula of *zeh chalifasi* must be altered to reflect the change. The wording would depend upon your choice of replacement item.

155   Unfortunately, the chaos associated with some commercial *kaparos* centers has at times become a point of contention between devotees and some local residents.

156   *Magen Avraham* §605:3.

157   *Mishnah Berurah* §605:6.

158   See *Mishnah Berurah* §605:6.

159   More on money in chap. 9, page 77.

Zeh Kaporosi

CHAPTER EIGHT

TZEDAKAH: REDEEMING THE CHICKENS AND DISTRIBUTING THEM TO *TZEDAKAH*

After using the chickens for *kaparos*, it is proper to continue to use them for other *mitzvos*.[160] In addition, by sharing the chicken with the poor, the person becomes more worthy of a *kaparah* and a *gemar tov*. Aside from the increased merit of the mitzvah, *tzedakah* specifically aids with achieving atonement. The Gemara[161] equates the merit of *tzedakah* with the annual half-*shekel* given to the Beis HaMikdash. Just as the half-*shekel* afforded the giver with *kaparah* via the *korbanos* it sponsored, similarly all *tzedakah* provides the donor with atonement.

Thus developed the ancient custom of distributing the *shechted* chickens to the poor.[162] Some *Rishonim*[163] opposed this practice, because it looks as if we are unloading our *aveiros*-ridden chickens on the hapless poor. Of course, this is not true. The chickens did not absorb any *aveiros* during the *kaparos* ceremony. However, the language used, "This is in my stead, this is my exchange," may lead the poor to feel that the chickens are laden with *aveiros*. Therefore, these *Rishonim* advocate that the participants themselves should eat the chickens and distribute money to the poor instead.

---

160   See *Shabbos* 117b, quoted in *Shulchan Aruch, O.C.* §394:2 and *Mishnah Berurah* §4.

161   *Bava Basra* 9b.

162   *Tur* §605.

163   *Maharil*, quoted in the *Rama* and *Magen Avraham* §605:4.

As a result, there are two *minhagim*: People give their chickens to the poor, or they eat their chickens themselves and contribute money to the poor. Today, most *kaparos* centers retain the chickens to distribute to the poor. Only a few return them, *kashered*, for the participants to take home.

When possible, try to take your chicken(s) home. Most *kaparos* centers cannot process all the chickens they *shecht* in one day, and inevitably more end up in the garbage than anybody would like to acknowledge. Taking them with you, even if you have to *kasher* them yourself, is a better option.[164] Most likely the *kaparos* center will be grateful to you for taking them home.

If your center allows you to take the *shechted* chicken home, verify that they will clean and *kasher* it first. If they give it to you *unkashered*, make sure that at least the internal inspection is done before you take it. (If a wound is discovered, you have still fulfilled the primary parts of the *minhag*—repentance and slaughter.) When you get home you should clean and *kasher* it according to the instructions in this manual.[165]

Once you have cleaned and *kashered* the chicken you may wish to distribute it directly to the destitute. While the poor certainly need money, providing actual food has advantages. When a poor person receives money, he must still go out and buy what he lacks. Giving him food (or other items) that he needs is a far greater mitzvah, because you eliminated one of the steps for him.[166]

---

164   For instructions on how to *kasher* a chicken at home, see the section "Home-Style *Kashering.*"
165   See chapter. 11, page 89 and Chapter 12, page 102.
166   *Mishnah Berurah* §605:5.

The Gemara[167] tells a story:

> Mar Ukva would regularly leave a coin by the home of a neighborhood pauper. One night, the poor man decided to discover the identity of his benefactor. On the night that the poor man lay in wait for him, Mar Ukva was delayed in the *beis ha-medrash*. His wife came to accompany him home. Along the way, they went together to drop the coin by the indigent's house. As they approached, Mar Ukva noticed the door move. Together with his wife, he ran and hid in an oven that had been cleared from its coals but was still quite hot. His feet started to burn, but his wife's did not. Mar Ukva was dismayed to discover that he was not as deserving of a miracle as his wife. She consoled him by pointing out that his merit for charity was limited because he was only able to supply the poor with money, while she, who stayed home and cooked, was able to supply the beggars with their real need—food. Thus, the merit of her charity was greater.

Your dollar, as beneficial as it is for the poor, is still a step removed from feeding them. *Kaparos* chickens provide immediate relief in the form of a meal.

Unfortunately, nowadays, this is not easily done. Most poor people will not take a chicken that you cleaned and *kashered* at home. They hope to receive a chicken that looks like it comes from a store; cut neatly and wrapped in cellophane. They also seek the assurance of a renowned distributing organization and a certifying agency to guarantee the sanitation and *kashrus* of the product. So you may have to redeem it by donating its value to the poor (currently about five U.S. dollars), while keeping the chicken for yourself.

Note: The cost of the *kaparos* (when the chicken itself is given to the poor) as well as the redemption money (when the chicken is not given directly to the poor) should be drawn

---

167   *Kesubos* 67b.

from personal funds and not from *maaser* money.[168] Although the money is used for *tzedakah* or other worthy causes, *kaparos*, like the *korban chatas*, is a required expense—חוב—and cannot be paid for with *maaser* funds.[169]

It is important that the redemption be done right away. Since giving the chicken or its substitute to the poor is an integral part[170] of the *kaparos* process, it should be attended to immediately. You also want to gain the extra merit of *tzedakah* before Yom Kippur. And of course, if it is not done right away there is the possibility that you may forget.

As a convenience for their customers, most *kaparos* centers, including those that allow you to take home the chickens, frequently factor a "redemption cost" into the price of the *kaparos*. This means that aside for paying them for the chicken you also already contributed extra money to go to the poor. Accordingly, you will not be required to redeem them when you get home. If you want to be sure, confirm with the organizers if this is the case.

---

168   *Maaser* funds—one-tenth of one's earnings, often designated as funds for charity or other *mitzvos*. According to many authorities this tithe is mandatory and the funds given towards it are not considered one's own assets. Therefore, they may not be used towards fulfilling one's monetary obligations.

169   *Mishnah Berurah* §605:6.

170   Although giving the money to *tzedakah* is integral to *kaparos*, it is only a secondary part of the process. Primary are *teshuvah* and *shechting* the bird, as will be explained in the following chapter.

Zeh Kaporosi

CHAPTER NINE

Using Money: An analysis of using money for *KAPAROS*

Nowadays, there are people who prefer to use money for *kaparos*, despite the ready availability of chickens. Using money may seem easier and cleaner, but can it be used to fulfill the *minhag*?

A few points to consider:

1. Since the founding of the *minhag* until modern times, the *minhag* has always been to use some sort of animal. Animals satisfy all six reasons (listed in Chapter 3) for which the *minhag* was instituted. Money does not fulfill any of them.

2. There is no mention of a custom to use money in any *sefer*.[171] Certainly, there were times when chickens were unavailable and money was the alternate *kaparah*—and this indeed is recorded in *sefarim*. However, money, when used, was only a temporary solution because there was no choice. It was never sanctioned as an official *minhag*.

3. In researching this *sefer*, I checked with Jews from all over prewar Europe to see if perhaps there was a *minhag* to use money in some part of Europe. I spoke to *Yidden* from Lita, Russia, Hungary, Poland, Romania, Austria, and even Germany. They all

---

171   A number of contemporary *sefarim* do include an option of using money. However, they never quote an earlier source, nor explain the purpose or gain to be had in using money. They are simply reporting what they see happening around them and do not mean to sanction a new custom. Their rationale in listing money will be explained below page 77 in the section, *"Origins of Using Money."*

told me that in their area chickens were used exclusively.[172] One *Yid* from Romania told me that in his poverty-stricken town the entire community lined up to share one chicken, but nobody thought to use money.

The *Chayei Adam*[173] is one of several *sefarim* which records the use of money in times of need. In the context of discussing inadequate *shechitos* he suggests it would be better to replace the chicken with money than to accept an inferior *shechitah*. However, in an ideal setting he is a strong advocate of using chickens for kaparos.

The *shochtim* of yore regularly trekked the countryside servicing the local Jews with *shechitah*. The night before Yom Kippur they trudged from village to village and house to house *shechting kaparos*-chickens. Because of the volume of homes to call on, the *shochtim* did not sleep that night. Many *Acharonim* worried that because of their *schlepping* and sleeplessness the *shochtim* would be too tired to inspect their knives carefully; with their heads heavy and senses dulled, they might overlook a nick in the knife. A flawed knife is invalid and the chicken *shechted* with it is a *nevielah*—carrion—and forbidden for consumption.

Many solutions were offered to resolve the problem: educating the *shochtim* better, spacing *kaparos* over a longer period and centralizing and supervising the *shechitah*, to mention a few. The *Chayei Adam* advocated abolishing *kaparos* in problem areas in order to eliminate the problem. He was upset by the people's indifference to the situation. They seemed reluctant to forgo the *minhag* despite the potential for producing *neveilos*. In desperation, he suggested replacing the chickens with money. He hoped that if the people retained some of the emotion of *kaparos* by using money they would be willing to abandon the chickens. He took inspiration for this idea from the existing paupers' habit of substituting expensive chickens with small money.

---

172   Actually, one woman from Cracow told me her grandfather, a fishmonger, would do *kaparos* for the family using a fish.

173   *Chayei Adam* §143:4, quoted by *Mishnah Berurah* §605:2.

The *Chayei Adam* does not recommend changing the *minhag* in the places where the *shechitah* is handled properly. In fact, further, in the same paragraph he praises people who had the means to have a *shochet* visit them specially and do an unrushed *shechitah*. He is only offering a solution for places where the *shechitah* was unsatisfactory. He felt it was better to abolish the *minhag* in those places and just observe a commemoration of it than to condone poor *shechitah* practices. Nowadays, when the *shechitah* at *kaparos* centers is controlled—the *Rabbanim* inspect the knives, decorum is maintained on the queue and the *shochtim* work unharassed for limited hours—there would be no reason to substitute money for the genuine *minhag*.

PEOPLE QUEUING UP FOR *SHECHITAH*

Neither the *Chayei Adam* nor anyone who quotes him says that the *minhag* of using chickens was ever altered. In fact, from his language it is clear that he did not see money as a fulfillment of the *minhag*. He only proffers it as an appeasement to the masses who are bent on doing *kaparos* at all costs, even when the *shechitah* was problematic.

THE *SHOCHET* IS SAFELY ENSCONCED IN HIS BOOTH. HERE HE CAN PLY HIS TRADE UNENCUMBERED. IN THE TOP PICTURE HE IS CALMLY INSPECTING HIS KNIFE. IN THE LOWER PICTURE HE IS ABLE TO *SHECHT* UNDISTURBED.

None of the later *Acharonim* say, "Now that we use money as the *Chayei Adam* recommended, this problem has been solved." On the contrary, there were *Acharonim* who, 200 years later, still felt it necessary to warn against poor *shechitah* practices. It is clear that in the interim the *minhag* had not been modified.

...The minhag of *kaparos* on Erev Yom Kippur has become established… Although many great authors wrote about this custom, what has become entrenched in the minds of the masses is that the atonement of Yom Kippur is dependent solely on this. People consider kaparos [a mitzvah] on par with eating matzah. They believe that only through their chicken will they attain *kaparah*. Because of this, in the large cities, there is shoving around the *shochtim*. Besides, the *shochtim* are sour and exhausted from their sleepless night.[174] They are incapable of inspecting their knives and there is a risk of eating *neveilah*—carrion. If those who wish to maintain this custom would seek my advice, I would recommend that they use money instead. Similar to what the commoners do when they cannot obtain a chicken. [Using money instead of a chicken] is comparable to the ancient custom of using a plant. Avoiding *neveilah* will be a great merit for them.

Even more so, when the proper custom (מנהג הנכון) is followed and the chickens, or their value, are distributed to the poor. Whoever can and wishes to do what is right (ורוצה מן המובחר), should arrange for the *shochet* to come [to his home] at dawn… But, he should not consider the chicken his atonement… (Chayei Adam §143:4)

Some people attempt to defend the practice of using money with the claim that at least *all* of the money goes to help the poor, whereas with chickens, besides the innards which are cast away, there is also a significant amount of money wasted on overhead.

However, *tzedakah* is only a secondary aspect of the *minhag*. The primary aim of *kaparos* is the thoughts of *teshuvah* with which one is inspired when watching the *shechitah*. The wording of the final phrase of the ceremony, "This chicken will go to its death…" indicates that *shechting* the bird is an integral part of the ritual. No mention is made of giving the bird or its worth to *tzedakah*.[175] Giving the chicken, or the redemption money,

---

174   In the more populated areas there was a large volume of work and the *shochtim* often had to work through the night.

175   Rav Eliyahu E. Dessler, *Michtav Me'Eliyahu Yom Kippur*, #541 (Appendix ל׳).

to the poor, although it adds merit and disposes of the chicken in a useful manner, is not the objective of *kaparos*.[176]

As mentioned above, there is no doubt that for a lack of chickens, the destitute of yesteryear used money. This included both impoverished families and the sons of well-to-do folks who were away at yeshiva. Elderly immigrants to America who had a specific way to wrap their few cents for *kaparos* were likely just copying what their poverty-stricken parents had done.

It is believed, though, that the new "custom" of using money for *kaparos* developed in America,[177] primarily because waving a chicken around one's head was perceived as unbecoming against the backdrop of modern American society. The migration of the chicken markets away from the cities, creating a scarcity of live chickens in Jewish population centers, also contributed to the shift toward using money. It is assumed that whoever pioneered the idea of money did so based on inspiration from the *Chayei Adam*. Under the circumstances, it was better to use money than allow such a precious custom to fall by the wayside.

However it came to be, by now there are a significant number of people who use money. Perhaps the option of using money has evolved into a new *minhag*?

To qualify as a *minhag,* the trend must be started by knowledgeable people for a *halachic* or *hashkafic* reason,[178] not for convenience. It must then be ratified by the *Rabbanim* of the next generations. Using money never achieved that status. On the contrary, all evidence indicates that the wide scale use of money was introduced in the United States for the reasons noted.

---

176   *Kaf HaChaim* §605:6.

177   Even in America, it seems to be a very late development. The Hebrew Publishing Company *machzor* did not include instructions for using money until the early 1960s. The first *machzor* to adapt the formula to accommodate money (from *tarnagol*—chicken—to *ma'mon*—money), was the Artscroll (August 1987).

178   See *Tosfos Pesachim* 51a (first on page).

Using chickens for *kaparos* is an ancient and universal custom. Through chickens one can attain the six benefits listed in Chapter 3.

There was a time and place that the *shechitah* was not managed properly. This problem was not widespread and was rectified long ago.

At one point a dearth of chickens and the perceived indecorousness of handling live birds caused some people to move away from chickens. This is no longer the case in the modern cities. *Kaparos* chickens are readily available and a wrangler[179] will gladly assist with the handling.

WRANGLERS HANDING OUT CHICKENS TO CUSTOMERS.

An additional advantage of chickens is the good it does for the destitute. As discussed in the previous chapter, when the chickens are distributed to the impoverished, the poor are one step closer to their meal.

Money, on the other hand, does not achieve any of the goals of *kaparos*. It has no historical precedent. Nor has anyone ever offered a rationale for the gain of waving coins over oneself.

It remains unquestionable that the authentic way to fulfill the *minhag* and retain all its benefits is by using live chickens. The use of money in lieu of *kaparos* is no more than a recent, artificial substitute of the *minhag*.

---

179   Wrangler—one who tends or cares for animals.

CHAPTER TEN

KISUY HADAM

What Each of Us Should Know about the Mitzvah

Kisuy hadam is a unique mitzvah that few people ever have the opportunity to fulfill. While the mitzvah is far from rare, it is seldom that the average person can participate in it. *Kisuy hadam*—the mitzvah of covering the blood of a bird or *chayah*[180] after *shechitah*— is usually done at distant, commercial poultry plants. It is only on occasions such as *kaparos,* when *shechitah* is arranged locally, that the common person can participate. It is therefore a mitzvah that, when accessible, generates a lot of excitement.

> **NOTE: THE TORAH CONCEPTS OF *BEHEIMAH* AND *CHAYAH* DO NOT NECESSARILY COINCIDE WITH THE COMMON OR SCIENTIFIC CLASSIFICATIONS OF ANIMALS AS WILD OR DOMESTICATED.**

Every time someone *shechts* a bird or a *chayah*, he must cover the blood with earth. What qualifies as earth? Soil does, of course, as does any other substance that plants can grow in, such as sawdust.

---

180   Which animals are called *chayos* and require *kisuy* and which are called *beheimos* and do not, will be covered below.

Earth in this context also includes anything the Torah calls earth, such as ash or finely ground gold.[181]

The blood must be covered from below and above. Before *shechting*, the *shochet* will scatter a kosher material, usually sawdust, on the ground near where he will *shecht*, and designate it for *kisuy hadam*. After the *shechitah*, he will allow some blood to collect on the sawdust, check his knife for nicks, and cover the blood with more sawdust.

SOME *BOCHURIM* REVIEWING THE *HALACHOS* OF *KISUY HADAM* WITH THE *SHOCHET*.

WHEN KAYIN KILLED HEVEL, THE GRIEVING ADAM STOOD BY THE CORPSE NOT KNOWING WHAT TO DO. SOME KOSHER BIRDS AND WILD ANIMALS CAME AND BURIED HEVEL. WE REPAY THEIR KINDNESS WHENEVER WE SLAUGHTER ONE OF THEIR KIND, BY BURYING ITS BLOOD.[1]

INGESTING BLOOD—THE FLUID OF LIFE—WOULD TURN US INTO AGGRESSIVE PEOPLE. TO HELP US RETAIN OUR DOCILE DISPOSITION, THE TORAH ENJOINS US FROM CONSUMING IT. TO FURTHER DISTANCE OURSELVES FROM AGGRESSIVENESS, WE ARE COMMANDED TO COVER THE BLOOD OF THE ANIMALS WE EAT.

IT IS NOT ALWAYS POSSIBLE TO COVER THE BLOOD OF A *BEHEIMAH*. WHEN A *BEHEIMAH* IS BROUGHT AS A *KORBAN*, ITS BLOOD MUST BE OFFERED ON THE *MIZBE'ACH* AND THEREFORE NOT BE COVERED. THEREFORE, THE TORAH LIMITED THIS REQUIREMENT TO BIRDS AND WILD ANIMALS.[2]

1   *Pirkei D'Rebbe Eliezer* 21; *Bereshis Rabbah* 22:8.
2   *Sefer Hachinuch* §187.

As mentioned, both birds and *chayos* require *kisuy*. We all know what birds are, but what are *chayos*? The Torah divides kosher mammals into two categories—*beheimos* and *chayos*. *Beheimos*, which do not require *kisuy hadam*, are frequently translated as domesticated animals. These are cattle, sheep, and goats. *Chayos*, often described as wild animals, do require *kisuy*.

Although the Gemara gives signs to identify a *chayah*, there are many

Zeh Kaporosi

181   The laws of *kisuy hadam* can be found in *Yoreh De'ah* §28.

SAWDUST PREPARED FOR *KISUY*.

THIS SETUP ELIMINATES ANY QUESTION ABOUT WHERE TO PUT THE DIRT. IT ALSO PUTS THE CUSTOMER AT RISK OF GETTING SPRAYED WITH BLOOD.

opinions among the *Rishonim* on how to understand these signs. It is therefore impossible to authoritatively identify an animal as a *chayah*. Accordingly, the *poskim*[182] say that we must have an oral tradition from rabbi to student to consider any animal a *chayah*. Otherwise, we must regard it as a questionable case and treat it with the stringencies of both a *chayah* and a *beheimah* (i.e., perform *kisuy*, but without a *berachah*[183]). Of the animals currently *shechted*, the fallow deer is known to be a *chayah* and the American bison (buffalo) is an example of an animal whose status is in question.

The basic mitzvah, to cover the blood from above and below with earth, is relatively easy to perform, and the majority of the *halachos* discussed in *Shulchan Aruch* cover unusual situations. We will now summarize the mitzvah as it is applied to the *kaparos* ritual.

Before he begins to *shecht*, the *shochet*—as described earlier—will set up a container with some sawdust or other dirt in it and designate the material for *kisuy hadam*. He will also set out

AFRICAN (WATER) BUFFALO. (NOTE THE SPLIT HOOVES.) THE *BEHEIMAH/CHAYA* STATUS OF THE BUFFALO IS DEBATED IN *SHULCHAN ARUCH*. THE *MECHABER* CONSIDERS IT A BEHEIMAH AND DOES NOT REQUIRE KISUY. THE *RAMA* CONSIDERS IT QUESTIONABLE AND REQUIRES *KISUY* WITHOUT A *BERACHAH*.

A FALLOW DEER BUCK. THE HORNLESS DOES (FEMALES) ARE FAMILIAR TO MANY WHO VACATION IN UPSTATE NEW YORK.

AMERICAN BUFFALO (BISON)

---

182   See *Shach Yoreh De'ah* §80:1.

183   *Shulchan Aruch Yoreh De'ah* §80:5. The *chelev* would also be *assur*, but that is beyond the scope of this discussion.

Chapter Ten

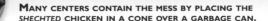

a bag of sawdust for the customer's convenience. The *shochet* will then *shecht* the chicken and place it in a cone over the dirt to collect the blood.

Who May Do *Kisuy?*

The Gemara says that *kisuy hadam* is the both the privilege and responsibility of the *shochet*. There is extensive debate among the *Acharonim* if the *shochet* may willingly pass up the opportunity to perform the mitzvah.[184] Our *minhag* is to permit someone other than the *shochet* to perform *kisuy hadam*. Therefore, frequently the *shochet* will honor the customer with the mitzvah.[185]

However, do not rush to do the mitzvah without receiving the *shochet*'s authorization. Since *kisuy hadam* is really the *shochet*'s mitzvah, it is proper to receive his explicit permission before covering the blood. The *shochet* must also check his knife for imperfections before a *berachah* can be said on the *kisuy*. It is appropriate to wait for the blood known as *dam hanefesh* to gather. There is an opinion that the *dam hanefesh* is the blood that comes out later. Therefore, you should not say the *berachah* until the *shochet* instructs you to do so.

Once the *shochet* gives his approval, gather a small amount of sawdust or other prepared soil in your hand, and prepare to say the *berachah*.

---

184   See *Shach Ch.M.* §382:4, *et al.*

185   See *Mateh Ephraim* §605:8, *Aruch Hashulchan* §28:16, and *Beis Dovid* §28 *Yesodei Habayis* 1–2.

Before saying the *berachah*, make sure that the area around you is free of foul odors and clear of chicken litter. In general, a chicken coop is considered unclean and a *berachah* may not be said in the immediate vicinity. Most *kaparos* centers look and smell every bit like a chicken coop.

Hold the soil in your hand while saying the *berachah*. If you pour the dirt on the blood before you say the *berachah*, your *berachah* will be superfluous—*berachah levatalah*.

The *berachah*:

בא"ה אמ"ה אקבמ"ו על מצות כיסוי דם בעפר.

Drop the soil where the *shochet* shows you to. Unfortunately, I have seen many people toss sawdust on the chicken instead of on the blood. If you do not cover the blood you have not performed the mitzvah.

As you drop the soil, your intention should be to cover the blood with earth in accordance with the mitzvah. You should also plan that this soil will be the "base-earth" for the next batch. If you did not do so, you can rely on the *shochet* to prepare it mentally, which is adequate, *be'dieved*.

You are not required to cover all the blood.[186]

THE *SHOCHET* IS SHOWING THE CUSTOMER WHERE TO PUT THE SAWDUST FOR *KISUY*.

---

186   For a full discussion on this topic see *Beis Dovid, Yesod Habayis* 28:9:1.

The *minhag* is not to say *Shehechiyanu* the first time you do *kisuy*. However, some like to prepare a fruit or other *shehechiyanu* item and say the *Shehechiyanu* on the *kisuy* with the fruit in mind.

CUSTOMERS OFTEN OMIT OR MISPRONOUNCE THE FINAL WORD בֶּעָפָר. A SIGN, LIKE THE ONE ON THE LEFT, SHOWING THE *BERACHAH* WITH THE *NEKUDOS* AIDS THE CUSTOMERS WITH GETTING IT RIGHT. THE SIGN ON THE RIGHT REMINDS THE CUSTOMERS OF THEIR COMMITMENT TO THE *SHOCHET*.

Remember:

1. Find an odor-free area to say the *berachah*.

2. Take the sawdust in your hand BEFORE beginning the *berachah*.

3. Say the *berachah*; THEN cover the blood.

4. Cover the blood, NOT the chicken.

5. *Shochtim* appreciate monetary TIPS.

THE DIRT OR SAWDUST FOR KISUY HADAM SHOULD BE PUT BETWEEN THE CONES.

CHAPTER ELEVEN

HOME-STYLE *KASHERING*: HOW TO *KASHER* A CHICKEN IN THE COMFORT OF YOUR HOME

(INCLUDING A "WHAT-YOU-NEED" LIST AND BASIC BUTCHERING INFORMATION)

IT IS TOLD THAT IN THE FORMER U.S.S.R., MANY HOUSEWIVES, ACCUSTOMED TO *KASHERING* THE MEAT THEY BROUGHT FROM THE *SHOCHET*, CONTINUED *KASHERING* EVEN WHEN KOSHER-SLAUGHTERED MEAT WAS NO LONGER AVAILABLE.

Kashering chickens in your home is an exciting and fulfilling experience. *Kashering* offers great educational opportunities and is not difficult to do. Yet, few families ever get the opportunity to do it. If you haven't yet tried *kashering* at home, it is strongly recommended that you consider doing so. You will be teaching your children about little-known *halachos* while you impart to them an important part of Jewish tradition. It is likely that your kids will eat more when they have watched the *kashering*. And besides, the food tastes better when you make it yourself!

Where to begin? You can start anywhere and anytime. Whether it is a chicken you brought home from *kaparos*, just some freshly *shechted* poultry, or even an exotic bird (with a *mesorah*[187]) you have come across.

---

187   *Mesorah*—tradition handed down through the generations, often concerning a particular interest (i.e., the identification of kosher birds) or the manner in which something is to be done.

Contrary to popular belief, *kashering* does not take much time, nor does it necessarily make a mess. The best part about it is that it does not require any specialized equipment. You can easily use common household items. With minimal preparation you can *kasher* one to a dozen chickens in your kitchen in just minutes.

Still, while the laws of *milichah*—salting—are essentially simple and easy to follow, it is possible that even a minor variance can be a major divergence. It is therefore important that you know and meticulously follow *hilchos milichah*.

An easy-to-use reference for the *halachos* of *kashering* is the *Kitzur Shulchan Aruch*.[188] This familiar classic is easy to read and understand. (The lengthy *Hilchos Milichah* found in *Shulchan Aruch Y. D.* deals almost entirely with the potential problems that can arise. Studying *Shulchan Aruch* also requires extensive background knowledge.)

Another thing you can do to avoid an accidental mishap is to set up your work environment properly.

The aim of this guide is to adapt one's working knowledge of *hilchos milichah* for today's kitchen. Thus, halachah and practical advice are intertwined without distinguishing between *halachic* requirement and efficiency. (In the event that a problem arises, consult a *rav* familiar with practical *milichah*.)

- These instructions assume that a proper inspection of the internal organs has already been made.

Zeh Kaporosi

---

188   *Siman 36.*

- All *kashering* should be done within 72 hours of the time of slaughter.[189]

- If the chicken was frozen, it must be thawed (without heat[190]) before *kashering*.

- Avoid using regular household pots and pans for the salting. This is because the utensils used in the *kashering* process are not to be used later for handling kosher food. Therefore, unless you have the funds and storage facilities for separate utensils, it is advisable to use disposables to the extent possible.

Here is a list of suggested materials to prepare before beginning the *kashering* process. You may substitute any item for a similar one you already have handy, or for one you think will do a better job.

A. Good-quality poultry scissors or very sharp knife

B. Disposable tablecloth

C. Heavy cardboard (e.g., cardboard box, egg box)

D. Garbage bags (optional)

E. Container larger than the chicken

KOSHER SALT IS COARSE SALT INTENDED SPECIFICALLY FOR PREPARING MEAT FOR KOSHER CONSUMPTION. FOR THE SALT TO WORK SUCCESSFULLY IT MUST CLING TO THE MEAT FOR THE DURATION OF THE KASHERING PERIOD WITHOUT DISSOLVING.

AS THE SALT PURGES THE BLOOD FROM THE MEAT, THE MEAT EXPELS FLUIDS. THE HALACHAH ALSO REQUIRES THAT THE MEAT BE DAMP AT THE START OF THE SALTING. TOGETHER, THESE LIQUIDS WOULD DISSOLVE A FINE SALT BEFORE IT HAS THE TIME TO DO ITS JOB.

ON THE OTHER HAND, LARGE SALT CRYSTALS WOULD NOT ADHERE TO THE MEAT. BECAUSE OF THEIR SIZE THEY WOULD BOUNCE OR OTHERWISE FALL OFF THE MEAT. THEREFORE, THE CORRECT SIZE TO USE FOR KASHERING IS A MEDIUM GRAIN. SEVERAL COMPANIES PRODUCE A SALT THAT MEETS THESE HALACHIC STANDARDS. THIS PRODUCT IS APTLY CALLED—KOSHER SALT.

---

189   After 72 hours from the time of *shechitah* the blood in the meat starts to thicken. The blood can no longer be removed with just soaking and salting. Only צלי—roasting/grilling can purge the blood after that point. Meat that was not *kashered* within 72 hours cannot be cooked, only roasted or grilled. (*Yoreh De'ah* §69:12, *Kitzur Shulchan Aruch* §36:27)

190   I.e., it cannot be defrosted in a microwave or with hot water.

F. Disposable plate

G. Kosher Salt (coarse salt, available in most grocery stores)

H. Perforated aluminum foil pan/new paint tray/old barbeque grate

I. Paper cup or spice bottle with sifter cap[191]

J. Kitchen timer (optional)

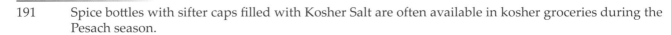

COMPARE THE COURSE KOSHER SALT ON THE LEFT TO THE FINER TABLE SALT ON THE RIGHT. MANY BRANDS PRODUCE BOTH KOSHER AND TABLE SALTS. EITHER CAN BE MADE FROM SALT ROCK (MINED) OR THE SEA.

SPICE BOTTLE WITH SIFTER CAP

Before *kashering* a chicken, you must do some basic butchering—just enough to make the chicken workable. There are many ways to prepare a chicken for *kashering*, most of them boring, tedious, tiring, and unsustainable in the long run. The method proposed here, admittedly, leaves the chicken a bit unsightly. On the other hand, it is easy and quick and you won't dread doing it again. In a proper work environment and with the right equipment, it should take about five minutes to prepare a chicken from *shechitah* to *kashering*.

I advocate removing the skin. However, some people prefer to pluck the feathers. They do not mind plucking and they like the "dressed look." If you opt to pluck feathers, you must complete the plucking before you begin butchering. If you choose to "pull the skin,"[192] you will do it in middle of the butchering process. This chapter is arranged in the order of when each activity is to be done: plucking first (in the box), basic butchering,

---

191   Spice bottles with sifter caps filled with Kosher Salt are often available in kosher groceries during the Pesach season.

192   "Pull the skin" is a technical term for removing the hide of a carcass.

followed by pulling skin, and finally the remainder of the butchering information.

NOTE: If you choose to pull the skin (recommended), then skip to the section on basic butchering.

TIP: If you have an outdoor workspace, then do the messy work (i.e., plucking and butchering) outdoors.

THE CLEANED (WELL, MAYBE NOT SO CLEANED, BUT AS CLEAN AS THE HOME-PLUCKER WILL GET IT,) CHICKEN LYING ON A CARDBOARD SHEET ON MY OUTDOOR TABLE. WORKING OUTDOORS ALLOWS ME TO KEEP THE MESS, (AND CLEANING CHICKENS CAN BE MESSY,) OUTSIDE. I FIND THAT CARDBOARD IS THE BEST MEDIUM TO WORK ON. IT STAYS PUT ON THE WORK SURFACE. THE CARDBOARD GRIPS THE CHICKEN AND PREVENTS IT FROM SLIDING AROUND. IT DOES NOT CLING TO THE CHICKEN AS PLASTIC OR PAPER WOULD. IT ALSO ABSORBS FLUIDS, SO THEY DO NOT SOIL THE FOOD.

PLUCKING

THE FEATHERS COME OUT EASIEST WHEN THE SKIN IS EITHER VERY WARM OR VERY COLD. NON-KOSHER FACILITIES HEAT THE SKIN WITH SCALDING WATER BEFORE PLUCKING THE FEATHERS. (THIS IS NOT AN OPTION FOR THE KOSHER-MINDED, BECAUSE SCALDING RENDERS THE CHICKEN UNFIT FOR *KASHERING*.) SOME KOSHER FACILITIES PASS THE CHICKENS THROUGH ICE WATER TO COOL THE SKIN BEFORE THE PLUCKING. THERE IS A SMALL WINDOW OF TIME, JUST AFTER *SHECHITAH*, WHEN THE CHICKEN IS STILL WARM AND THE FEATHERS WILL COME OFF EASILY. PULL THEM GENTLY IN THE DIRECTION WHICH THE FEATHERS POINT. IF YOU PULL HARD OR IN THE WRONG DIRECTION YOU MAY TEAR THE SKIN.

TIP: SOME PEOPLE REPORT THAT IT IS EASIER TO PULL THE FEATHERS IF THEY ARE WET. SO YOU MAY WANT TO SOAK THE CHICKEN IN (ICE) COLD WATER FOR A FEW MINUTES BEFORE YOU START PLUCKING.

Basic Butchering (Both Methods)

1. Bend the leg at the knee[193] and cut through the cartilage of the joint. (It is much easier to cut cartilage than bone.)

2. Cut at a 45-degree angle. Always cut on the side of the joint you plan to discard.

3. Do the same for the second leg and both wings. Cut the wings at the joint closest to the body.[194]

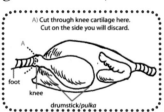

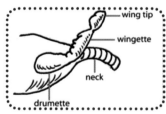

PREPARING TO REMOVE THE FEET AND WINGS. BEND THE FOOT AT THE JOINT. PLAN TO CUT EXACTLY IN THE MIDDLE OF THE YELLOW KNOB.

Method Two: Pulling Skin

4. Now remove the skin. To do so, make an incision in the skin near the neck and pull the skin from the back. The skin comes off most of the chicken easily. The breast area is easiest.

   The back is a little harder—particularly near the spine. When

USE A GOOD QUALITY POULTRY SCISSORS (AVAILABLE IN ALL HOUSEWARE STORES) OR A SHARP KNIFE TO SLICE THROUGH THE JOINT. NOTICE THAT THE CUT IS IN THE MIDDLE OF THE JOINT, NOT ABOVE OR BELOW IT. CUTTING THROUGH THE CENTER OF THE JOINT IS MUCH EASIER, AND THE RESULTS MUCH NICER, THAN CUTTING THROUGH THE BONE.

---

193   Anatomically this joint is more like an ankle than a knee. Its correct name is hock joint. However, most people think of it as the knee.

194   Too much effort is needed to prepare the extra parts of the wing.

you get to the ends of the wings or legs pull hard and smoothly. Although, you might need a little extra energy to pull the skin at some of these tips, do not be tempted to yank the skin off harshly. Doing so will tear the skin and make it harder to remove the remainder.

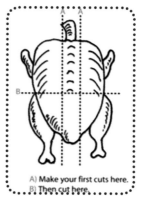

A) Make your first cuts here.
B) Then cut here.

5. Place (the skinned) chicken, breast down, on the cardboard. Make two cuts down the back of the chicken on either side of the spine, from the top (neck area) through the thighs down until the tail. (Lines A in diagram.)

START FROM THE NECK AREA AND CUT ALONG THE SPINE.

CUT STRAIGHT DOWN THE BACK.

CUT ALONG THE OTHER SIDE OF THE SPINE. REMOVE SPINE AND DISCARD.

REMOVE TAIL (OIL GLANDS).

6. Cut between the thighs and the back/breast to separate the top from the bottom. (Line B in diagram on previous page.) You now have three pieces; the breasts, the thighs and the spine/back.

7. Remove and discard the spine/back with the neck and all the organs intact. (For *kaparos*, the innards should be thrown on the roof, or at least in an area accessible to wild animals—provided your neighbors don't mind.)

Some people save the backs and necks for making soup. In that case,

To continue cutting the chicken into quarters, lift it by the leg and cut between the "top" and "bottom."

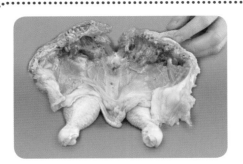

The opened chicken. Bits of lungs and the kidneys are visible.

they will have to detach all the organs from the back and kasher it along with the rest of the chicken.

Removing the organs will be much easier, now that you have separated the back from the rest of the chicken.

You now have three manageable pieces of chicken (the breasts and two thighs).

TRIM AWAY THE SHARP EDGES OF THE RIBS.

THE PREPARED BREASTS

THE THREE USABLE PIECES OF CHICKEN; THE TOP (IN ONE PIECE) AND THE BOTTOMS (QUARTERED)

8. Rinse the chicken with cold water and clean it the way you normally would for cooking.

9. When the chicken is clean and all visible blood has been removed, set chicken to soak in clean room temperature/ cool water. (Tap water from the cold faucet is fine.) Quart size disposable (pickle) containers or 9"×13" foil pans are ideal. Alternatively, you can line a household bucket or garbage pail and soak the chickens in those containers.

THE COAGULATED BLOOD VISIBLE BENEATH THE SKIN (ON THE BENDS OF THE WINGS) IN THIS AND SEVERAL OTHER PICTURES WILL DISSOLVE AND DISAPPEAR WHEN THE CHICKEN IS SOAKED.

The container used for soaking is known as a *veich-schissel* (softening basin), and should not be used for processing ordinary kosher food.

10. The water must cover the entire chicken. Sometimes a piece of chicken will float to the surface and become partly exposed. It should be pushed back into the water.

TIP:

- Line the container with a plastic bag before filling with water. Then tie the bag just above the water.

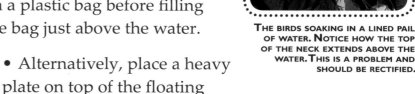

THE BIRDS SOAKING IN A LINED PAIL OF WATER. NOTICE HOW THE TOP OF THE NECK EXTENDS ABOVE THE WATER. THIS IS A PROBLEM AND SHOULD BE RECTIFIED.

- Alternatively, place a heavy plate on top of the floating chicken to keep it in the water.

NOTE: SOME COMMERCIAL PROCESSORS USE A TREMENDOUS AMOUNT OF SALT. THIS REMOVES ALL COLOR FROM THE CHICKEN AND WHEN COOKED, THE BONES AND SINEWS ARE WHITE. HOME *KASHERING* USES LESS SALT AND DOES NOT REMOVE ALL THE COLOR FROM THE CHICKEN. WHEN COOKED, THE BONES AND SINEWS ARE SOMETIMES BLACK.

11. After putting the last piece of chicken into the water, mark down the time. This is the "start time." Wait thirty minutes. (You can track the time by setting the kitchen timer.)

12. If you are using a foil pan as a *zalts-brettal* (salting-board), then prepare the pan while the chicken is soaking. Punch holes through the bottom with a knife. Twist the knife slightly in each hole to widen it just a bit. Depress the center of the pan slightly so the secretions will be able to drain. Spread cardboard or a disposable tablecloth on the counter beneath the pan to catch the drips of blood-laden brine, so that they do not make the counter *treif*. Set the pan upside down on the tablecloth.

FOIL PAN RECAST AS *ZALTS-BRETTAL*

Zeh Kaporosi

13. When the half hour is up, remove the chicken pieces from the water. Examine the surface of the meat for any coagulated blood. Let the water run off, but do not allow the chicken to dry.[195]

14. Place the still-damp chicken, one piece at a time, on a disposable plate and sprinkle with Kosher (coarse) Salt.[196]

A. Fill a paper[197] cup with Kosher Salt and uniformly spread a thin layer of salt to cover all six sides of the chicken. Pinch the cup to control the flow of salt. Use gentle, even motions to systematically cover every area of the chicken with a thin layer of salt. Alternatively, you can use an old spice container with a sifter cap to distribute the salt.

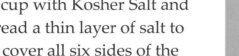

MAKE SURE TO GET ALL SIDES OF EVERY PIECE. LIFT WINGS AND OTHER PARTS TO GET THEIR UNDERSIDE AND BENEATH THEM

Pay special attention to the edges and crevices.

B. When doing many chickens at one time, you may find it easier to just fill a

> **BENEFITS OF SALTING WITH A SPICE CONTAINER WITH SIFTER CAP:**
> - **EASIER TO COVER HARD-TO-REACH SPOTS**
> - **EASILY GETS SALT INTO CREVICES**
> - **COVERS EVENLY, WITH LESS SALT**
> - **SALT WON'T IRRITATE FINGERS**
> - **SALT STAYS DRY**
> - **DOESN'T WASTE SALT**

---

195   There is a practical reason for this halachah. The salt will bounce off the dry meat. There must be some moisture to catch the salt and make it stick.

196   When doing a large bird (i.e., a whole turkey or goose) or if you work slowly, you must work on a perforated surface, so that the secretions will not collect.

197   Use a paper cup. It is hard to pinch a plastic cup well.

large pan with salt and coat the chicken with salt as you would do with breadcrumbs.

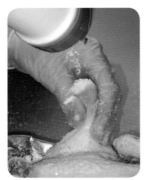

CUTTING AWAY THE LOOSENED SKIN MAKES *KASHERING* EASIER.

C.   If you left the skin on, make sure to salt underneath any loose flaps of skin.

15.   Once the chicken has been salted, set it on the rack, paint tray, or inverted perforated pan. (When using a paint tray, secure the chicken high on the tray so that it does not slip down into the secreted juices.)

16.   When the last piece has been salted, set kitchen timer or mark down the time. Wait one hour.

17.   When the hour is up, rinse all the pieces under cold running water to remove any residual salt. Then dip each piece into a pan of fresh water. Change the water and repeat.

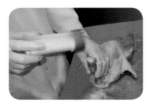

DON'T FORGET TO DO THE TIPS.

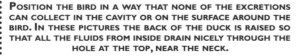

POSITION THE BIRD IN A WAY THAT NONE OF THE EXCRETIONS CAN COLLECT IN THE CAVITY OR ON THE SURFACE AROUND THE BIRD. IN THESE PICTURES THE BACK OF THE DUCK IS RAISED SO THAT ALL THE FLUIDS FROM INSIDE DRAIN NICELY THROUGH THE HOLE AT THE TOP, NEAR THE NECK.

SAFELY AWAY FROM THE EXCRETED BRINE. THE DISPOSABLE PLATE IN THIS PICTURE IS CATCHING THE BRINE. THIS BRINE IS *TREIF*. WERE IT TO DRIP ON THE COUNTER OR OTHER UTENSIL THOSE ITEMS WOULD BECOME *TREIF*.

A PILE OF SALTED QUAILS. THE MEAT MAY BE STACKED AS THE SALT DOES ITS JOB. NOTICE THAT THEY ARE ARRANGED IN A MANNER THAT PREVENTS LIQUID FROM GATHERING INSIDE OR BETWEEN THEM. THEY ARE ALSO POSITIONED SAFELY AWAY FROM THE ACCUMULATING BRINE.

18. Change the water and re-dip a third time. During this final wash, allow the pieces to soak for a few minutes to remove much of the absorbed salt, lowering the sodium content and improving the taste.

The chicken is now salted and kosher. You may now prepare it any way you like.

CHAPTER TWELVE

MORE ON *KASHERING*: HOW TO *KASHER* THE REST OF THE CHICKEN, OTHER METHODS, AND *KASHERING* UNCOMMON BIRDS

How to open the gizzard (*pupikal*) without making a mess:

The *pupikal* is shaped like a flattened ball with an opening at the top and side. At the core of the gizzard is a pouch containing undigested food. It is wisest to remove and discard this bag intact. You will have to cut through the outer muscle and peel it off the inner sac. The key is to cut through the muscle without opening this pouch. If the sac is opened, the waste inside will soil your food.

> **IT IS EASIER TO PEEL THE GIZZARD WHEN IT IS COLD. PLACE IT IN THE FREEZER WHILE YOU PREPARE THE REST OF THE CHICKEN.**

To open the gizzard safely, use a circular sawing motion to gently cut along the side from the top opening towards the bottom. Use caution as you get deeper into the muscle, and stop short of the center.

THE PUPIK (GIZZARD) WITH THE PROVENTRICULUS STILL ATTACHED. THE CHICKEN'S PUPIK IS COMPARABLE TO A STOMACH. FOOD ENTERS THE GIZZARD THROUGH THE PROVENTRICULUS, IS GROUND, AND EXITS THROUGH THE OTHER SMALLER HOLE ON THE SIDE. THE *PUPIK* ITSELF IS SHAPED SOMEWHAT LIKE AN OVAL DISC, WITH ROUNDED SIDES AND FLAT ON TOP AND BOTTOM.

Pull the last bit apart with your hands and remove the lining intact. *Kasher* as you would any other meat.

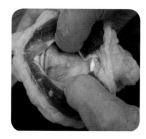

USE A SHARP KNIFE AND CUT AROUND THE OUTER SIDE. STOP JUST BEFORE THE INNER SAC.

THE MUSCLE HAS BEEN CUT THROUGH AND THE INNER SAC IS STILL INTACT. WITH A FIRM MOTION PULL THE REMAINDER OF THE MUSCLE APART.

SLOWLY PEEL THE EDIBLE MEAT OFF THE INNER SAC.

Livers

Chicken livers are easy to *kasher*. They don't need to be cleaned, nor do they need a lengthy soak or an extended salting. Just rinse, broil, and rinse again. The broiler does all the work for you.[198]

- Rinse the livers. Add a dash of Kosher Salt and broil. Grill them on a disposable barbeque grill or put them into your broiler until done. Rinse them three times.[199]

---

198   Chicken livers do not need to be cut before kashering because a) they are small, and b) they rip when they're removed from the rest of the organs.

199   *Kitzur Shulchan Aruch* §36:20.

Chapter Twelve

- *If* you wish to cook[200] the livers (after *kashering*) you may remove them from the grill after just a few minutes, once the inside is edible (the entire outside is dry).

PLUCKING TIPS:

- IT IS EASIEST TO PLUCK FEATHERS WHEN THE CHICKEN IS STILL WARM; FOR THIS REASON YOU ARE IN A BIT OF A HURRY TO START.
- SOME PEOPLE FIND THE OPPOSITE TO BE EASIER. THEY SOAK THE CHICKEN IN ICE WATER FOR A FEW MINUTES. (ALL AGREE THAT IT IS MOST DIFFICULT AT ROOM TEMPERATURE.)
- SOME PEOPLE REPORT THAT IT IS EASIER TO PULL THE FEATHERS IF THEY ARE WET.
- WHEN PLUCKING, START FROM THE NECK AREA AND WORK YOUR WAY DOWN. STAY AWAY FROM THE BOTTOM OF THE BACK WHERE THE OIL GLANDS ARE. IT IS MUCH HARDER TO PLUCK THE FEATHERS ONCE YOUR FINGERS GET OILY.
- BE GENTLE! IT IS HARDER TO PLUCK AND *KASHER* IF THE SKIN IS RIPPED.

- When broiling, you must place the meat on a grate or perforated pan so that the meat will not sit in the secreted juices.

- Generally, it is not practical to *kasher* just one chicken liver. However, since you must broil it anyway, you are not in a rush to *kasher* within 72 hours.[201] You can save up a number of livers in the freezer until you have enough to make it worth the effort.

NOTE: The *minhag* is not to eat the liver or gizzard of the *kaparos* chickens.[202]

---

200   Cooking in this context includes all forms of cooking (i.e., boiling, frying, sautéing…), aside from grilling/broiling.

201   Livers, like any meat that was not *kashered* within 72 hours, cannot be cooked after *kashering*. See footnote 192 above.

202   See chap. 4, "Discarding the Innards."

Alternative Kashering Methods

BROILING

Prepare the chicken as you would for cooking. Scatter a little salt on the meat and grill or broil it until edible. Rinse three times with cold water.[203]

When broiling, you must place the meat on a grate or perforated pan so that the meat will not sit in the secreted juices.

WHOLE CHICKENS

Chickens can also be *kashered* whole with the skin on. However, it is much harder, messier, and time consuming. Still, those who like to stuff their chickens need them whole. Other birds, such as duck, turkey and quail, are usually *kashered* and cooked whole.

1. Pluck the feathers and wash away all visible blood Remove the organs from the cavity. Pay special attention to the little bits of lung that get stuck between the ribs. Some also remove the kidneys from their hiding spot beneath the membrane covering them inside of the thighs.

Brown Quail (Coturnix coturnix)

YOU ARE NOW READY TO OPEN THE CHICKEN AND REMOVE THE GUT. LOCATE THE TIP OF THE BREAST AND CUT RIGHT BELOW IT. BE GENTLE AND GO SLOW. IF YOU CUT DEEPLY YOU MAY SEVER THE GUTS.

  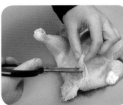  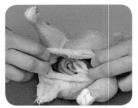

EASY DOES IT. MAKE SMALL CUTS.	START WITH A SMALL HOLE LIKE THIS.	WIDEN IT SLOWLY.	THIS IS ABOUT AS WIDE A HOLE YOU WANT TO CUT.	NOW PULL IT THE REST OF THE WAY APART BY HAND.

THE GUT HAS BEEN REMOVED AND THE INTERIOR CLEANED.
AT THE FRONT OF THE PICTURE ON THE LEFT IS A NICE LUMP OF *SCHMALTZ*. IF YOU LIKE *SCHMALTZ* THEN LEAVE IT INTACT AND KASHER IT ALONG WITH THE REST OF THE CHICKEN. IF YOU DON'T APPRECIATE *SCHMALTZ* THEN REMOVE AND DISCARD IT NOW. NOTICE HOW THE EXTENDED LEFT LEG CREATES A HOLLOW. YOU MUST SALT ALL SIDES OF THE INTERIOR OF THIS POCKET. AN EASY WAY TO ACCESS THIS AREA (AND ELIMINATE THE POCKET) IS BY MAKING A SMALL SLIT IN THE SKIN AS INDICATED IN THE PICTURE.

2. Slit the skin that is holding the thighs to the main body of the chicken. This will slightly spoil the appearance of the finished product, but it will be much easier to *kasher*.

TIP:

A KITCHEN SPRAY HOSE, FOUND ON MANY SINKS, OR A DISPOSABLE PLASTIC KNIFE CAN BE VERY HELPFUL IN REMOVING THE STUBBORN BITS OF DIRT, BLOOD, BONE, LUNGS, AND KIDNEYS.

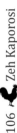

3. Remove or cut the two blood vessels in the neck. Old-timers prefer to remove them, but it is difficult for the beginner to locate them, so just make two or three round cuts across the front and side of the neck. The cuts should be long, deep and spaced, so that you can be sure that you cut into the veins.[204]

THE EXPOSED NECK. THE WHITE STREAK IN THE CENTER (PARTLY COLORED RED) IS THE VEIN THAT MUST BE REMOVED. THE OTHER WHITE STREAKS, ABOVE AND BELOW, ARE THE NECK LIGAMENTS.

PULL THE VEIN GENTLY, BUT FIRMLY TO REMOVE IT. (IF IT RIPS, IT IS TREATED AS CUT, WHICH IS ALSO ACCEPTABLE.)

A QUAIL WITH THE VEIN CLEARLY VISIBLE.

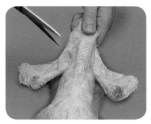

ANOTHER OPTION IS TO REMOVE THE NECK ALTOGETHER. AIM TO CUT AS CLOSE TO THE BASE AS POSSIBLE.

I PREFER THE LAST OPTION, BECAUSE NECKS ARE HARD TO KASHER. YOU NEED TO SALT BENEATH THE PEELED SKIN, WHICH CAN BE CUMBERSOME. WITH THE NECK OUT OF THE WAY YOU HAVE BETTER ACCESS TO THE AREAS AROUND THE BASE OF THE NECK. BESIDES, WHAT CAN BE DONE WITH A KASHERED CHICKEN'S NECK?

4. Soak the chicken as described above (steps 9–15).

5. Start salting from the inside. Sprinkle salt from your "spice-bottle," aiming to cover every exposed spot. (Some people find it easier to salt the inside

THE CLEANED AND SOAKED BIRD. YOU ARE NOW READY TO START SALTING. IT IS WISE TO BEGIN SALTING INSIDE THE CAVITY.

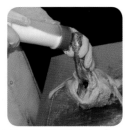

IT IS ALWAYS EASIEST TO SALT THE INSIDE FIRST. AIM YOUR SALT INTO THE CAVITY FROM THE OPENINGS ON TOP AND BOTTOM.

---

204   At times a small amount of congealed, dark-purple, residual blood may be visible in these veins.

by hand.) Begin from the bottom of the cavity (innermost section) and work up towards the front. Turn the chicken over to do the top of the interior.

6. Then do the outside. Be careful to cover every area. Don't miss the folds and beneath the flaps of loose skin.[205]

LOOSE SKIN CAN BE A CHALLENGE. YOU MUST LIFT THE EDGE IN ORDER TO GET THE SALT BENEATH IT.

SALT THE REMAINDER OF THE BIRD.

A SALTED DUCK.

7. When done, set the chicken breast-side-down on the *zalts-brettal*.[206] The chicken should be positioned in a way that liquid cannot gather in the cavity.

• The chicken can also be hung from a strong, wire clothes hanger over a lined garbage can. Insert the hanger into the cavity of the chicken with the hook coming out of the top (neck area). A duck or turkey may require more than one hanger.

Continue from step 18 above.

A DUCK HANGING BY A WIRE HANGER FROM A ROD. THERE IS A LINED WASTEBASKET BELOW IT TO CATCH THE DRIPPINGS.

Whole vs. Cut

There is an ongoing debate if it is preferable to *kasher* chickens whole or quartered. Both methods are *halachically* acceptable. Either one may be

---

205   One of the benefits of *kashering* chickens whole is that there are fewer angles to cover and considerably less loose skin than quartered chickens.

206   See step 14 above on how to prepare a *zalts-brettal*.

Zeh Kaporosi

used by the conscientious homemaker. The question is which system can be followed more efficiently by people who do their job by rote.

The issues revolve around hard-to-reach areas and loose skin.

Whole chickens have their skin intact with barely any loose edges. The surfaces are smooth and completely accessible. There are no hidden areas that need to be salted.

However, it can be difficult to clean small bits of residual organs and occasional dirt from inside the cavity. (This matter must be removed before salting.) This problem affects the novice more than the skilled preparer. The beginner is more likely to rip organs and drop dirt during evisceration.

Salting inside the partially closed cavity can also be difficult. It can be hard to manipulate where the salt will fall. There is a possibility that salt may not reach the neck side (anterior[207]) of the cavity or between the ribs. While this problem can affect anyone, it is more pronounced with inexperience.

Quartered or even open[208] chickens have no cavity to contend with. Cleaning and salting the limbs are much easier. The downside is that there are large flaps of dangling loose skin which must be *kashered* on both sides. Once the skin is cut, the area around the edges often detaches from the meat. The peeling skin must be lifted and both the surface of the meat and the underside of the skin must be salted. Cutting the

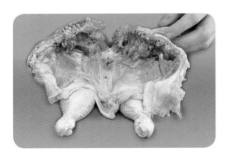

THIS IS HOW A "*KASHERED* **OPEN" CHICKEN LOOKS (ALBEIT A LITTLE CLEANER) BEFORE SALTING.**

---

207   Anterior—of or near the head or toward the front of a body.
208   Open—industry jargon for a chicken that has been split along the spine, from the neck area on top until the tail area on bottom. It is short for "open back *kashering*."

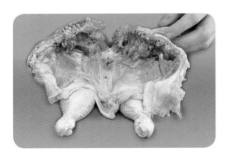

chicken apart exposes nooks and crannies that did not previously exist. These must now be *kashered*.

Kashering chickens whole requires greater expertise. *Kashering* cut chickens demands greater presence of mind.

In my opinion this debate is limited to commercial operations—systems that employ calloused, often non-Jewish or non-religious, workers. Since they put little or no thought into what they are doing, there is a need for a failsafe system. The occasional home-*kasherer* who will pay attention to every detail, will likely have an easier time cleaning and salting a skinned and quartered chicken.

	Whole		Quartered, Open	
	Pros	Cons	Pros	Cons
1.	Intact skin	Bits of organs and dirt left in the cavity	No cavity	Must be salted between the skin and the top of the meat
2.	Smooth and accessible surfaces	Hard to salt in cavity	Easier to clean and salt	Flaps of loose skin that must be *kashered* on two sides
3.	No hidden areas			Many exposed nooks and crannies that must *kashered*

CHAPTER THIRTEEN

TEHILLIM KAPITEL 107, IYOV 33

In this chapter, we will explore *Tehillim* 107 and *Iyov* 33. These *kapitlach* are the sources for the *pesukim* recited during *kaparos*. Each of these fascinating *kapitlach* will first be explained in context, using the standard *mefarshim* of the *Mikro'os Gedolos*. Then the *pesukim* from these chapters which are actually said during *kaparos* will be explained in light of how they are used.

The message of both sets of *pesukim* is that Hashem's ways are just. Hashem never afflicts a person with more than he deserves. Hardship and difficulty are the products of man's own doing. If it has been decreed on High that a person suffer death, he must justly deserve it.

An important precept of *Yiddishkeit* is to accept misfortune as punishment for misdeeds (*tziduk hadin*) and follow up with a confession of wrongdoings (*viduy*). The story of King Yoshiyahu succinctly illustrates these concepts.

King Yoshiyahu had disobeyed the *navi* when he set out with his army to block Paraoh Necho, King of Egypt, from passing through Eretz Yisrael. The Egyptian archers quickly put three hundred arrows through King Yoshiyahu's body. As he lay dying of his wounds, he accepted Hashem's punishment and declared, "צדיק הוא ה' כי פיהו מריתי— Hashem is righteous, for I had violated His command."[209] Similarly, during every Jewish

Zeh Kaporosi

---

209   *Medrash Eichah* 1:53.

funeral, a prayer declaring the righteousness of Hashems' judgment is read. The prayer is aptly called *Tziduk Hadin*.

The Mishnah[210] teaches that even a convicted sinner is to be given the opportunity to confess before being put to death. After the defeat of Yericho, Yehoshua saw fit to consecrate all the captured booty; violators were to be executed. One man, Achan, stole from the hallowed materials. As Achan was being led to his death, Yehoshua urged him to confess. Yehoshua told Achan that by acknowledging his sin he will earn a place in the World to Come.

Not only those guilty of a capital offense must repent; every person needs

DID YOU KNOW?

KAPITEL, MEANING CHAPTER, WAS YIDDISHIZED FROM THE LATIN CAPITALE. MEDIEVAL SCRIBES, AND LATER, PRINTERS, MARKED THE BEGINNING OF A NEW CHAPTER WITH A LARGE LETTER. THE CAPITALE, OR CAPITAL AS WE CALL IT, BECAME SYNONYMOUS WITH A NEW CHAPTER. THE ORIGINAL PRINTERS OF THE TANACH THOUGHT IT WOULD BE A GREAT IMPROVEMENT IF THEY WOULD "ENHANCE" IT WITH THE CHURCH'S PURELY ARBITRARY CHAPTER BREAKS. THUS, THE EARLY TANACHS WERE PRINTED WITH THE CHRISTIAN NUMBERING SYSTEM. THE SYSTEM, ALTHOUGH IMPOSED UPON US, SPREAD QUICKLY AND STUCK FAST. ALL SUBSEQUENT ATTEMPTS TO MODIFY IT WERE UNSUCCESSFUL.

TO DIFFERENTIATE BETWEEN AUTHENTIC BREAKS, LIKE CHAPTERS OF GEMARA, AND ARBITRARY ONES, LIKE BIBLICAL CHAPTERS, THE FORMER ARE CALLED BY THE HEBREW WORD FOR BREAK—PEREK AND THE LATTER ARE KNOWN BY THEIR LATIN, ALBEIT YIDDISHIZED, NAME—KAPITEL.

---

210   *Sanhedrin* 43b.

to confess before he dies. Thus, the terminally ill are encouraged to confess and hopefully attain atonement before they die.[211]

During the *aseres yemei teshuvah,* when all of man's deeds are considered and his future hangs in the balance, it is natural for one to be concerned about his verdict. There exists the real possibility of an unfavorable decree. To forestall the execution of such a judgment against him, he chooses a chicken—a *kaparah*—to "replace" him. To impress himself with the earnestness of the situation, before slaughtering the chicken, he recites *pesukim* that parallel both the *Viduy*-confession, and *Tziduk Hadin,* said after death. The *pesukim* emphasize that it is man's sins that cause his suffering and it is only through *teshuvah*—returning to Hashem—that he can save himself.

Tehillim Kapitel 107   תהלים קעפטעל קז

This kapitel expresses the gratitude of those rescued from harm. They thank Hashem for the challenge as well as for their salvation. Hardships are how Hashem alerts the offender to the peril of his behavior. Without difficulties, a person might blindly blunder through life perpetuating his errors. The pesukim focus on the travails of the four groups who are required to bentch gomel (ארבעה צריכים להודות)*: travelers who have returned from the (1) desert or (2) sea, (3) captives who have been released, and (4) patients who have recuperated.*

These four groups are more aware of the precariousness of their situation than most others who have suffered harm. Having experienced the dangers firsthand, their call to teshuvah and subsequent gratitude are most sincere.

211   *Shulchan Aruch Yoreh De'ah* §338:1.

Desert Travelers

[1,2] Those who have been saved from difficulties must praise Hashem. They must declare, "Hashem is constantly good." [3,4] Travelers who have returned from the far-flung corners of the earth; disoriented, they wandered aimlessly in the desert, their path did not cross civilization. [5] As they meandered, they exhausted their food, they hungered. [6,7] After they realized the error of their ways—they contemplated why had Hashem sent them on this long and arduous journey? Why did they lose their way, if not to call attention to their iniquities? They repented and prayed, so Hashem returned them to civilization. [8] They must tell the world about the chesed Hashem did for them-[9] He fed them and did not allow them to perish in their sins.

(א) הֹדוּ לַה' כִּי טוֹב כִּי לְעוֹלָם חַסְדּוֹ: (ב) יֹאמְרוּ גְּאוּלֵי ה' אֲשֶׁר גְּאָלָם מִיַּד צָר: (ג) וּמֵאֲרָצוֹת קִבְּצָם מִמִּזְרָח וּמִמַּעֲרָב מִצָּפוֹן וּמִיָּם: (ד) תָּעוּ בַמִּדְבָּר בִּישִׁימוֹן דָּרֶךְ עִיר מוֹשָׁב לֹא מָצָאוּ: (ה) רְעֵבִים גַּם צְמֵאִים נַפְשָׁם בָּהֶם תִּתְעַטָּף: (ו) וַיִּצְעֲקוּ אֶל ה' בַּצַּר לָהֶם מִמְּצוּקוֹתֵיהֶם יַצִּילֵם: (ז) וַיַּדְרִיכֵם בְּדֶרֶךְ יְשָׁרָה לָלֶכֶת אֶל עִיר מוֹשָׁב: (ח) יוֹדוּ לַה' חַסְדּוֹ וְנִפְלְאוֹתָיו לִבְנֵי אָדָם: (ט) כִּי הִשְׂבִּיעַ נֶפֶשׁ שֹׁקֵקָה וְנֶפֶשׁ רְעֵבָה מִלֵּא טוֹב:

Prisoners

[10,11] For violating the word of G-d and shunning His desires, they were shackled and fettered in the dark. They sat in the shadow of death. [12] Hashem chastened them with hopeless difficulties. [13, 14] As a result, they called to Hashem and were spared. [15] They are to proclaim that Hashem treats people with amazing kindness. [16]For He crushed the copper gates and axed the iron latches [of the prison].

(י) יֹשְׁבֵי חֹשֶׁךְ וְצַלְמָוֶת אֲסִירֵי עֳנִי וּבַרְזֶל: (יא) כִּי הִמְרוּ אִמְרֵי אֵ-ל וַעֲצַת עֶלְיוֹן נָאָצוּ: (יב) וַיַּכְנַע בֶּעָמָל לִבָּם כָּשְׁלוּ וְאֵין עֹזֵר: (יג) וַיִּזְעֲקוּ אֶל ה' בַּצַּר לָהֶם מִמְּצֻקוֹתֵיהֶם יוֹשִׁיעֵם: (יד) יוֹצִיאֵם מֵחֹשֶׁךְ וְצַלְמָוֶת וּמוֹסְרוֹתֵיהֶם יְנַתֵּק: (טו) יוֹדוּ לַה' חַסְדּוֹ וְנִפְלְאוֹתָיו לִבְנֵי אָדָם: (טז) כִּי שִׁבַּר דַּלְתוֹת נְחֹשֶׁת וּבְרִיחֵי בַרְזֶל גִּדֵּעַ:

Illness

[17] Fools, who did not repent as illness slowly overtook them, until they became deathly ill. [18] Their sins caused them to suffer until the point that they could no longer eat. [19] When they called to Hashem, He redeemed them from their troubles. [20] He rescued them from their destructive path. [21, 22] They are to bring gifts of thanksgiving and publicly sing Hashem's praise.

(יז) אֱוִלִים מִדֶּרֶךְ פִּשְׁעָם וּמֵעֲוֹנֹתֵיהֶם יִתְעַנּוּ: (יח) כָּל אֹכֶל תְּתַעֵב נַפְשָׁם וַיַּגִּיעוּ עַד שַׁעֲרֵי מָוֶת: (יט) וַיִּזְעֲקוּ אֶל ה' בַּצַּר לָהֶם מִמְּצֻקוֹתֵיהֶם יוֹשִׁיעֵם: (כ) יִשְׁלַח דְּבָרוֹ וְיִרְפָּאֵם וִימַלֵּט מִשְּׁחִיתוֹתָם: (כא) יוֹדוּ לַה' חַסְדּוֹ וְנִפְלְאוֹתָיו לִבְנֵי אָדָם: (כב) וְיִזְבְּחוּ זִבְחֵי תוֹדָה וִיסַפְּרוּ מַעֲשָׂיו בְּרִנָּה:

Sea Farers

[23] People whose sinful ways prevented them from earning a living locally, were forced to sail to distant lands. [24] At sea, they witnessed Hashem's majesty firsthand. [25] Hashem called up a storm and they were tossed about. [26, 27] They keeled like drunken sailors, their sailing skills useless, until their hearts melted. [28] They realized the need to repent and turned to Hashem. [29] The sea calmed and the waves returned to whispers. [30] They enjoyed calm seas as they were pleasantly led to their destination. [31] They must admit that Hashem treats people kindly. [32] They must praise Him in front of the multitudes, in the presences of the elders.

(כג) יוֹרְדֵי הַיָּם בָּאֳנִיּוֹת עֹשֵׂי מְלָאכָה בְּמַיִם רַבִּים: (כד) הֵמָּה רָאוּ מַעֲשֵׂי ה' וְנִפְלְאוֹתָיו בִּמְצוּלָה: (כה) וַיֹּאמֶר וַיַּעֲמֵד רוּחַ סְעָרָה וַתְּרוֹמֵם גַּלָּיו: (כו) יַעֲלוּ שָׁמַיִם יֵרְדוּ תְהוֹמוֹת נַפְשָׁם בְּרָעָה תִתְמוֹגָג: (כז) יָחוֹגּוּ וְיָנוּעוּ כַּשִּׁכּוֹר וְכָל חָכְמָתָם תִּתְבַּלָּע: (כח) וַיִּצְעֲקוּ אֶל ה' בַּצַּר לָהֶם וּמִמְּצוּקֹתֵיהֶם יוֹצִיאֵם: (כט) יָקֵם סְעָרָה לִדְמָמָה וַיֶּחֱשׁוּ גַּלֵּיהֶם: (ל) וַיִּשְׂמְחוּ כִי יִשְׁתֹּקוּ וַיַּנְחֵם אֶל מְחוֹז חֶפְצָם: (לא) יוֹדוּ לַה' חַסְדּוֹ וְנִפְלְאוֹתָיו לִבְנֵי אָדָם: (לב) וִירֹמְמוּהוּ בִּקְהַל עָם וּבְמוֹשַׁב זְקֵנִים יְהַלְלוּהוּ׃

Conclusion

[33] Hashem can cause drastic changes. Rivers can turn to desert and springs to parched land. [34] Fertile land can become barren because of the evil of the inhabitants. [35] If it is His will, deserts can develop oases and forsaken lands can sprout springs. [36, 37] Cities can be built to house the destitute, and fields and vineyards planted to feed them. [38] They will be blessed and flourish. Their flocks will not diminish.

(לג) יָשֵׂם נְהָרוֹת לְמִדְבָּר וּמֹצָאֵי מַיִם לְצִמָּאוֹן: (לד) אֶרֶץ פְּרִי לִמְלֵחָה מֵרָעַת יֹשְׁבֵי בָהּ: (לה) יָשֵׂם מִדְבָּר לַאֲגַם מַיִם וְאֶרֶץ צִיָּה לְמֹצָאֵי מָיִם: (לו) וַיּוֹשֶׁב שָׁם רְעֵבִים וַיְכוֹנְנוּ עִיר מוֹשָׁב: (לז) וַיִּזְרְעוּ שָׂדוֹת וַיִּטְּעוּ כְרָמִים וַיַּעֲשׂוּ פְּרִי תְבוּאָה: (לח) וַיְבָרֲכֵם וַיִּרְבּוּ מְאֹד וּבְהֶמְתָּם לֹא יַמְעִיט׃

[39] But, the sinners are brought down and diminished. [40] Disgrace is heaped upon the evil leaders; they are displaced. [41] While the [refined] poor are elevated and multiplied.

(לט) וַיִּמְעֲטוּ וַיָּשֹׁחוּ מֵעֹצֶר רָעָה וְיָגוֹן: (מ) שֹׁפֵךְ בּוּז עַל נְדִיבִים וַיַּתְעֵם בְּתֹהוּ לֹא דָרֶךְ: (מא) וַיְשַׂגֵּב אֶבְיוֹן מֵעוֹנִי וַיָּשֶׂם כַּצֹּאן מִשְׁפָּחוֹת׃

[42] The just take notice and are gladdened, while evil is silenced.

(מב) יִרְאוּ יְשָׁרִים וְיִשְׂמָחוּ וְכָל עַוְלָה קָפְצָה פִּיהָ:

[43] The wise must be attentive to this and contemplate Hashem's ways.

(מג) מִי חָכָם וְיִשְׁמָר אֵלֶּה וְיִתְבּוֹנְנוּ חַסְדֵי ה':

Of the four groups listed in this *kapitel,* the *pesukim* of only two, the prisoners and the ill, are included in the *kaparos*-ceremony. Only when discussing these two cases does the *pasuk* specifically mention that their suffering is a result of the person's sins. Furthermore, it is abundantly clear to all that these two misfortunes must be the work of G-d in retribution for ones wrongdoings. For only G-d, and not man himself, can bring imprisonment or illness.[212]

Background to Iyov 33:23,24 [213]

Throughout the *sefer,* Iyov, who has suffered terribly, grapples with the concept of suffering. Starting in *kapitel* 31, Iyov wonders: Is he not an extremely righteous person; why should he suffer? He challenges his three friends, Bildad Hashochi, Tzophar Hanamasi, and Elifaz Hatemani to explain why he suffers so.

Iyov states his case in very strong terms: (31:3-6) "Is not calamity for the perverse person; and disaster for those who commit iniquity? Were Hashem to weigh me on the scales of righteousness, He would know my integrity! (7, 8) Have I ever taken something from another, that my produce be taken by plunderers? (13, 14) Have I ever spurned the justice of my servant or of my maidservant when they contended with me—then I would have no answer when Hashem rises against me. (16, 17) Have I withheld from the poor, or caused the eyes of the widow to fail? Have I eaten my bread alone, and not shared it with an orphan? (24-26) Have I made gold my hope, have I said to the fine gold: 'You are my confidence'? Did I wish to serve the sun when it shone, or the moon in

---

212   *Minhagei Yeshurun,* 149 (page 82), Rabbi Avrohom Eliezer Hirshowitz, Vilna 5659.
213   The excerpted *pesukim* have been translated interpretively.

its brightness? (35) Who will hear me? My desire is that Hashem should answer me. Let my accuser write a book against me." He continues in this vein for many *pesukim*.

(32:1) His three friends are speechless. Iyov has effectively established his righteousness. They are unable to offer a reasonable response.

(2-6) Elihu son of Barachel from the family of Buzi [son of Nochur[214]], a relative of Avraham Avinu, who is not one of the original three friends, accepts the challenge. He answers on behalf of Hashem.

He begins, (33:8-13) "Why do you suspect Hashem of injustice? Would you accuse a man of unwitting harm? Is Hashem less calculated than a reasonable mortal? (14) Hashem calls a person to *teshuvah* once or twice. (19) If the man is unresponsive, than Hashem must afflict him; slowly drawing him to toward the grave. (23-24) If he has to his credit even one good deed, than an intercessor angel would vouch for him. Hashem would graciously rescue the person from his hardships, accepting the one good deed as ransom."

Elihu asserts that Hashem is truly just. The punishments He metes out are commensurate with the iniquity of the violator: (34:12) "Surely G-d will not do wickedly, neither will the Almighty pervert justice. (21) For His eyes are upon the ways of a man, and He sees all his goings. (27) Because they turned aside from following Him, and did not contemplate all His ways. (10) Therefore, hearken to me men of understanding. Far be it from G-d, that He should do wickedness and from the Almighty, that He should commit iniquity. (11) Rather, He repays the deeds of man, and causes every man to [come upon difficulties] according to his conduct."

Zeh Kaporosi

---

214   *Metzudas David.*

Elihu continues in this vein for many *pesukim*. Starting in *kapitel* 38, Hashem addresses Iyov. Hashem's answer runs for four *kapitlach* and builds on Eilhu's words.

Two of these *pesukim* (33:23-24) are included in the *kaparos* ceremony.

Seder Kaparos—סדר כפרות

נֶפֶשׁ תַּחַת נֶפֶשׁ

A soul[1] in place of a soul.[2]

בְּנֵי אָדָם, יֹשְׁבֵי חֹשֶׁךְ וְצַלְמָוֶת אֲסִירֵי עֳנִי וּבַרְזֶל:

Children of man:[3] Cowering in the dark shadow of death, painfully bound in chains.

אֱוִילִים מִדֶּרֶךְ פִּשְׁעָם וּמֵעֲוֹנֹתֵיהֶם יִתְעַנּוּ: כָּל אֹכֶל תְּתַעֵב נַפְשָׁם וַיַּגִּיעוּ עַד שַׁעֲרֵי מָוֶת:

Fools[4] did not repent as illness slowly overtook them, until they became deathly ill. Their sins caused them to suffer until the point that they could no longer eat.

וַיִּזְעֲקוּ אֶל ה׳ בַּצַּר לָהֶם מִמְּצֻקוֹתֵיהֶם יוֹשִׁיעֵם: יִשְׁלַח דְּבָרוֹ וְיִרְפָּאֵם וִימַלֵּט מִשְּׁחִיתוֹתָם:

When they call to Hashem, He redeems them from their troubles. With His will He cures them;[5] He rescues them from [the consequences of] their destructiveness.[6]

יוֹדוּ לַה׳ חַסְדּוֹ וְנִפְלְאוֹתָיו לִבְנֵי אָדָם:

They are to tell[7] among people[8] of Hashem's kindness and wonder.

אִם יֵשׁ עָלָיו מַלְאָךְ מֵלִיץ אֶחָד מִנִּי אָלֶף לְהַגִּיד לְאָדָם יָשְׁרוֹ: וַיְחֻנֶּנּוּ וַיֹּאמֶר פְּדָעֵהוּ מֵרֶדֶת שַׁחַת מָצָאתִי כֹפֶר:

If, despite a thousand failures, one *malach* will vouch for him,[9] Hashem will save him. Hashem will be gracious to him and declare, "Save him from descending to the Pit, I have found redemption."

Zeh Kaporosi

After reciting the *pesukim*, the chicken is waved overhead while saying the appropriate passage:

---

1. MEN SAY:

This is my exchange, this is my replacement, this is my atonement.	זה חליפתי, זה תמורתי, זה כפרתי.
The death of this rooster will substitute for my death,	זה התרנגול ילך למיתה,
and I will be preserved[10]	ואני אכנס
for a good, long life and to peace.[11]	לחיים טובים וארוכים ולשלום.

---

2. SEVERAL MEN SHARING ONE CHICKEN SAY:

This is our exchange, this is our replacement, this is our atonement.	זה חליפתנו, זה תמורתנו, זה כפרתנו.
The death of this rooster will substitute for our death,	זה התרנגול ילך למיתה,
and we will be preserved	ואנו נכנס
for a good, long life and to peace.	לחיים טובים וארוכים ולשלום.

---

3. WHEN PERFORMING THE RITUAL FOR A MAN:

This is your exchange, this is your replacement, this is your atonement.	זה חליפתך, זה תמורתך, זה כפרתך.
The death of this rooster will substitute for our death,	זה התרנגול ילך למיתה,
and you will be preserved	ואתה תכנס
for a good, long life and to peace.	לחיים טובים וארוכים ולשלום.

4. WHEN PERFORMING THE RITUAL FOR SEVERAL MEN:

This is your exchange, this is your replacement, this is your atonement.	זה חליפכם, זה תמורתכם, זה כפרתכם.
The death of this rooster will substitute for your death,	זה התרנגול ילך למיתה,
and you will be preserved	ואתם תכנסו
for a good, long life and to peace.	לחיים טובים וארוכים ולשלום.

5. WOMEN SAY:

This is my exchange, this is my replacement, this is my atonement.	זאת חליפתי, זאת תמורתי, זאת כפרתי.
The death of this hen will substitute for my death,	זאת התרנגולת תלך למיתה,
and I will be preserved	ואני אכנס
for a good, long life and to peace.	לחיים טובים וארוכים ולשלום.

6. SEVERAL WOMEN SHARING ONE CHICKEN SAY:

This is our exchange, this is our replacement, this is our atonement.	זאת חליפתנו, זאת תמורתנו, זאת כפרתנו.
The death of this hen will substitute for our death,	זאת התרנגולת תלך למיתה,
and we will be preserved	ואנו נכנסו
for a good, long life and to peace.	לחיים טובים וארוכים ולשלום.

7. WHEN PERFORMING THE RITUAL FOR A WOMAN SAY:

This is your exchange, this is your replacement, this is your atonement.	זאת חליפתך, זאת תמורתך, זאת כפרתך.
The death of this hen will substitute for your death,	זאת התרנגולת תלך למיתה,
and you will be preserved	ואת תכנסי
for a good, long life and to peace.	לחיים טובים וארוכים ולשלום.

8. WHEN PERFORMING THE RITUAL FOR SEVERAL WOMEN (SHARING ONE CHICKEN) SAY:

This is your exchange, this is your replacement, this is your atonement.	זאת חליפתכן זאת תמורתכן, זאת כפרתכן.
The death of this hen will substitute for your death,	זאת התרנגולת תלך למיתה,
and you will be preserved	ואתן תכנסנה
for a good, long life and to peace.	לחיים טובים וארוכים ולשלום.

9. A PREGNANT WOMAN PERFORMING THE RITUAL FOR HERSELF SAYS:

According to the instructions in the *machzorim* a pregnant woman should take two or three chickens in her hand at once and say:

These are our exchange, these are our replacement, these are our atonement.	אלו חליפתנו, אלו תמורתנו, אלו כפרתנו.
The death of these hens will substitute for our death,	אלו התרנגולים ילכו למיתה,
and we will be preserved	ואנו נכנסו
for a good, long life and to peace.	לחיים טובים וארוכים ולשלום.

If it is not possible to hold all of them together, she should take one at a time, saying first for herself and then for the child.

This is my exchange, this is my replacement, this is my atonement.	זאת חליפתי, זאת תמורתי, זאת כפרתי.
The death of this hen will substitute for my death,	זאת התרנגולת תלך למיתה,
and I will be preserved	ואני אכנס
for a good, long life and to peace.	לחיים טובים וארוכים ולשלום.

Then she should take a second hen for the possible daughter and say:

This is your exchange, this is your replacement, this is your atonement.	זאת חליפתך, זאת תמורתך, זאת כפרתך.
The death of this hen will substitute for your death,	זאת התרנגולת תלך למיתה,
and you will be preserved	ואת תכנסי
for a good, long life and to peace.	לחיים טובים וארוכים ולשלום.

When using two chickens she should take one hen and say:

These are our exchange, these are our replacement, these are our atonement.	אלו חליפתנו, אלו תמורתנו, אלו כפרתנו.
The death of these hens will substitute for our death,	זאת התרנגולת תלך למיתה,
and we will be preserved	ואנו נכנסו
for a good, long life and to peace.	לחיים טובים וארוכים ולשלום.

For the possible son she should take one rooster and say:

This is your exchange, this is your replacement, this is your atonement.	זה חליפתך, זה תמורתך, זה כפרתך.
The death of this rooster will substitute for our death,	זה התרנגול ילך למיתה,
and you will be preserved	ואתה תכנס
for a good, long life and to peace.	לחיים טובים וארוכים ולשלום.

10. WHEN PERFORMING THE RITUAL FOR A PREGNANT WOMAN SAY:

If it is possible, take two or three chickens together and say:

These are your exchange, these are your replacement, these are your atonement.	אלו חליפתיכם, אלו תמורתיכם, אלו כפרתיכם.
The death of these chickens will substitute for your death,	אלו התרנגולים ילכו למיתה,
and you will be preserved	ואתם תכנסו
for a good, long life and to peace.	לחיים טובים וארוכים ולשלום.

If it is not possible to hold all the chickens together; when using three chickens, take one hen for the woman and say as below. Then take the second hen for the possible daughter and repeat:

This is your exchange, this is your replacement, this is your atonement.	זאת חליפתך, זאת תמורתך, זאת כפרתך.
The death of this hen will substitute for your death,	זאת התרנגולת תלך למיתה,
and you will be preserved	ואת תכנסי
for a good, long life and to peace.	לחיים טובים וארוכים ולשלום.

Then take a rooster and say:

This is your exchange, this is your replacement, this is your atonement.	זה חליפתך, זה תמורתך, זה כפרתך.
The death of this rooster will substitute for our death,	זה התרנגול ילך למיתה,
and you will be preserved	ואתה תכנס
for a good, long life and to peace.	לחיים טובים וארוכים ולשלום.

When using just two chickens, take one hen and say:

These are your exchange, these are your replacement, these are your atonement.	אלו חליפתיכם, אלו תמורתיכם, אלו כפרתיכם.
The death of these chickens will substitute for your death,	אלו התרנגולים ילכו למיתה,
and you will be preserved	ואתם תכנסו
for a good, long life and to peace.	לחיים טובים וארוכים ולשלום.

Then take the rooster and say:

This is your exchange, this is your replacement, this is your atonement.	זה חליפתך, זה תמורתך, זה כפרתך.
The death of this rooster will substitute for our death,	זה התרנגול ילך למיתה,
and you will be preserved	ואתה תכנס
for a good, long life and to peace.	לחיים טובים וארוכים ולשלום.

While saying these words, the penitent should focus on what is about to happen to his chicken. The chicken's death at the hands of the *shochet* represents the four penalties of *Beis Din*. Thus, he should be thinking, "It is as if I were being killed for my sins. The tightened neck skin is as if I were to be strangled—*chenek*, the knife symbolizes *hereg*, throwing the bird to the ground after *shechitah* corresponds to stoning—*sekilah*, singing the feathers (when cleaning the fowl), or cooking the bird correlates to *sereifah*.[215]

---

215   *Mateh Ephraim* §605:5.

A person who cannot hold the chicken for himself may have someone else revolve the chicken over his head. If possible, the penitent should recite the *pesukim* and *zeh chalifasi*. When not possible, someone else may say the *pesukim* and *zeh chalifasi* on their behalf. The wording of *zeh chalifasi* will need to be adjusted to match the situation.

1   *A soul*—נפש is often translated as soul. Here it is being used in its less common connotation—body, or living organism. Some versions actually read גופו תחת גופך. Its body replaces your body (Sefer Haminhagim-Tirnau-Aseres Yemei Teshuvah), or גבר תחת גָבר—gever for a gever (Sefer Haminahgim-Maharam-Seder Yom Kippur).

2   *A soul in place of a soul*—Many sources include this declaration of what the penitent is about to do, in the *kaparos* ceremony. Some put it in the beginning while others add it later before זה חלפתי. He is declaring that the chicken is to take his place. Any harm that was to befall the man shall befall the chicken instead. The concept is based on the *Medrash Pesikta*—א״ר יצחק בנוהג שבעולם אדם נכשל בעבירה והוא מתחייב עליה מיתה לשמים, מת שורו, אבדה תרנגולתו, נשברה צלוחיתו, ניכשל באצבעו, מקצת הנפש ככל הנפש—Rabbi Yitzchak said, "It would be expected that if a person sinned he should be castigated with capital punishment. [However,] if his ox dies, his chicken is lost, his pitcher breaks, or he injures a finger—part of the soul is like the entire soul [i.e., the loss of the item has excused him]." A premise of *kaparos* is that the chicken should serve as a substitute for the person should he be due any punishment.

3   *Children of man*—These words do not appear in the present *pasuk*, nor in the very early versions of the ceremony. They do appear several times in this *kapitel*, in both earlier and later *pesukim* (8, 15, 21, 31). They are included in the *kaparos* text of the later *Rishonim*. It is unclear by whom and when they were added, or what message they are to convey. They may simply be introductory words. Since the *pesukim* do not appear in their original context it was necessary to add an opening phrase. It is possible they were added in order not to open with an unpleasant expression, יושבי חושך—*Cowering in the dark* (Machzor Ohalei Yakov).

4   *Fools*—*Tehillim* refers to the sick as fools. Poor health is the result of sin. A person who sinned and succumbed to illness has behaved foolishly (*Ibn Ezra*).
      Generally, people do not get sick suddenly. Illnesses start as a minor problem and progress. Hashem first tries to attract the person's attention with a minor ailment. But the person pays no heed; he persists in his evil ways. So Hashem is forced to intensify the degree of illness until the person is bedridden, then unable to eat, and finally approaches death. Now, he understands the severity of his actions and is ready to do *teshuvah*. He was a fool, because he should have taken notice and corrective action with the first sign of ill health (*Radak*). Additionally, they are fools because they do not view illness as a message from Hashem. They ascribe their situation to nature (*Malbim*).

5   *With His will*—Hashem cures with His will alone. Unlike a doctor, He has no need for elixirs and potions (*Radak*).

6   *Their destructiveness*—The evil of their ways would have brought them to the brink of death. (*Radak*)

7   *They are to tell.* The redeemed must thank Hashem publicly for His salvation. (*Metzudas David*)

8   *Among people*—Alternatively, these words can be explained, that although from Hashem's perspective these feats are no big deal, we humans see them as mind-boggling. The *pasuk* thus reads, "They must express thanks to Hashem for what seems to us as amazing feats of kindness and astonishment." (*Malbim*)

9   *One* malach *will vouch*—A protecting *malach* is created with every mitzvah done. (*Avos* 4:12) Had the person done even one mitzvah, his *malach* would intercede on his behalf. He would merit salvation for just that one deed.

10   *And I*—It is important to pause before the word "ואני—And I" and not after it. It should not sound like he is saying, "This chicken shall go to its death and I (too)."

11   *Peace*—Peace is the most important of all *berachos*. Most other *berachos* lose their significance in the absence of peace. אין כלי מחזיק ברכה אלא שלום (במדבר רבה (וילנא) פרשת פינחס פרשה כא. (*Machzor Ohalei Yakov*)

HEBREW SOURCES

א. איוב קאפיטל לב-לג

(קאפיטל לב) (ב) וַיִּחַר אַף אֱלִיהוּא בֶן בַּרַכְאֵל הַבּוּזִי מִמִּשְׁפַּחַת רָם בְּאִיוֹב חָרָה אַפּוֹ עַל צַדְּקוֹ נַפְשׁוֹ מֵאֱלֹהִים: (ג) וּבִשְׁלֹשֶׁת רֵעָיו חָרָה אַפּוֹ עַל אֲשֶׁר לֹא מָצְאוּ מַעֲנֶה וַיַּרְשִׁיעוּ אֶת אִיּוֹב: (ד) וֶאֱלִיהוּ חִכָּה אֶת אִיּוֹב בִּדְבָרִים כִּי זְקֵנִים הֵמָּה מִמֶּנּוּ לְיָמִים: (ה) וַיַּרְא אֱלִיהוּא כִּי אֵין מַעֲנֶה בְּפִי שְׁלֹשֶׁת הָאֲנָשִׁים וַיִּחַר אַפּוֹ: פ

(ו) וַיַּעַן אֱלִיהוּא בֶן בַּרַכְאֵל הַבּוּזִי וַיֹּאמַר צָעִיר אֲנִי לְיָמִים וְאַתֶּם יְשִׁישִׁים עַל כֵּן זָחַלְתִּי וָאִירָא מֵחַוֺּת דֵּעִי אֶתְכֶם: (ז) אָמַרְתִּי יָמִים יְדַבֵּרוּ וְרֹב שָׁנִים יֹדִיעוּ חָכְמָה: (ח) אָכֵן רוּחַ הִיא בֶאֱנוֹשׁ וְנִשְׁמַת שַׁדַּי תְּבִינֵם: (ט) לֹא רַבִּים יֶחְכָּמוּ וּזְקֵנִים יָבִינוּ מִשְׁפָּט: (י) לָכֵן אָמַרְתִּי שִׁמְעָה לִּי אֲחַוֶּה דֵּעִי אַף אָנִי: (יא) הֵן הוֹחַלְתִּי לְדִבְרֵיכֶם אָזִין עַד תְּבוּנֹתֵיכֶם עַד תַּחְקְרוּן מִלִּין: (יב) וְעָדֵיכֶם אֶתְבּוֹנָן וְהִנֵּה אֵין לְאִיּוֹב מוֹכִיחַ עוֹנֶה אֲמָרָיו מִכֶּם: (יג) פֶּן תֹּאמְרוּ מָצָאנוּ חָכְמָה אֵל יִדְּפֶנּוּ לֹא אִישׁ: (יד) וְלֹא עָרַךְ אֵלַי מִלִּין וּבְאִמְרֵיכֶם לֹא אֲשִׁיבֶנּוּ: (טו) חַתּוּ לֹא עָנוּ עוֹד הֶעְתִּיקוּ מֵהֶם מִלִּים: (טז) וְהוֹחַלְתִּי כִּי לֹא יְדַבֵּרוּ כִּי עָמְדוּ לֹא עָנוּ עוֹד: (יז) אַעֲנֶה אַף אֲנִי חֶלְקִי אֲחַוֶּה דֵעִי אַף אָנִי: (יח) כִּי מָלֵתִי מִלִּים הֱצִיקַתְנִי רוּחַ בִּטְנִי: (יט) הִנֵּה בִטְנִי כְּיַיִן לֹא יִפָּתֵחַ כְּאֹבוֹת חֲדָשִׁים יִבָּקֵעַ: (כ) אֲדַבְּרָה וְיִרְוַח לִי אֶפְתַּח שְׂפָתַי וְאֶעֱנֶה: (כא) אַל נָא אֶשָּׂא פְנֵי אִישׁ וְאֶל אָדָם לֹא אֲכַנֶּה: (כב) כִּי לֹא יָדַעְתִּי אֲכַנֶּה כִּמְעַט יִשָּׂאֵנִי עֹשֵׂנִי:

(איוב קאפיטל לג) (א) וְאוּלָם שְׁמַע נָא אִיּוֹב מִלָּי וְכָל דְּבָרַי הַאֲזִינָה: (ב) הִנֵּה נָא פָּתַחְתִּי פִי דִּבְּרָה לְשׁוֹנִי בְחִכִּי: (ג) יֹשֶׁר לִבִּי אֲמָרָי וְדַעַת שְׂפָתַי בָּרוּר מִלֵּלוּ: (ד) רוּחַ אֵל עָשָׂתְנִי וְנִשְׁמַת שַׁדַּי תְּחַיֵּנִי: (ה) אִם תּוּכַל הֲשִׁיבֵנִי עֶרְכָה לְפָנַי הִתְיַצָּבָה: (ו) הֵן אֲנִי כְפִיךָ לָאֵל מֵחֹמֶר קֹרַצְתִּי גַם אָנִי: (ז) הִנֵּה אֵמָתִי לֹא תְבַעֲתֶךָּ וְאַכְפִּי עָלֶיךָ לֹא יִכְבָּד: (ח) אַךְ אָמַרְתָּ בְאָזְנָי וְקוֹל מִלִּין אֶשְׁמָע: (ט) זַךְ אֲנִי בְּלִי פָשַׁע חַף אָנֹכִי וְלֹא עָוֺן לִי: (י) הֵן תְּנוּאוֹת עָלַי יִמְצָא יַחְשְׁבֵנִי לְאוֹיֵב לוֹ: (יא) יָשֵׂם בַּסַּד רַגְלָי יִשְׁמֹר כָּל אָרְחֹתָי: (יב) הֵן זֹאת לֹא צָדַקְתָּ אֶעֱנֶךָּ כִּי

יִרְבֶּה אֱלוֹהַּ מֵאֱנוֹשׁ: (יג) מַדּוּעַ אֵלָיו רִיבוֹתָ כִּי כָל דְּבָרָיו לֹא יַעֲנֶה: (יד) כִּי בְאַחַת יְדַבֶּר אֵל וּבִשְׁתַּיִם לֹא יְשׁוּרֶנָּה: (טו) בַּחֲלוֹם חֶזְיוֹן לַיְלָה בִּנְפֹל תַּרְדֵּמָה עַל אֲנָשִׁים בִּתְנוּמוֹת עֲלֵי מִשְׁכָּב: (טז) אָז יִגְלֶה אֹזֶן אֲנָשִׁים וּבְמֹסָרָם יַחְתֹּם: (יז) לְהָסִיר אָדָם מַעֲשֶׂה וְגֵוָה מִגֶּבֶר יְכַסֶּה: (יח) יַחְשֹׂךְ נַפְשׁוֹ מִנִּי שָׁחַת וְחַיָּתוֹ מֵעֲבֹר בַּשָּׁלַח: (יט) וְהוּכַח בְּמַכְאוֹב עַל מִשְׁכָּבוֹ וריב עֲצָמָיו אֵתָן: (כ) וְזִהֲמַתּוּ חַיָּתוֹ לָחֶם וְנַפְשׁוֹ מַאֲכַל תַּאֲוָה: (כא) יִכֶל בְּשָׂרוֹ מֵרֹאִי ושפי עַצְמוֹתָיו לֹא רֻאּוּ: (כב) וַתִּקְרַב לַשַּׁחַת נַפְשׁוֹ וְחַיָּתוֹ לַמְמִתִים: (כג) אִם יֵשׁ עָלָיו מַלְאָךְ מֵלִיץ אֶחָד מִנִּי אָלֶף לְהַגִּיד לְאָדָם יָשְׁרוֹ: (כד) וַיְחֻנֶּנּוּ וַיֹּאמֶר פְּדָעֵהוּ מֵרֶדֶת שַׁחַת מָצָאתִי כֹפֶר: (כה) רֻטֲפַשׁ בְּשָׂרוֹ מִנֹּעַר יָשׁוּב לִימֵי עֲלוּמָיו: (כו) יֶעְתַּר אֶל אֱלוֹהַּ וַיִּרְצֵהוּ וַיַּרְא פָּנָיו בִּתְרוּעָה וַיָּשֶׁב לֶאֱנוֹשׁ צִדְקָתוֹ: (כז) יָשֹׁר עַל אֲנָשִׁים וַיֹּאמֶר חָטָאתִי וְיָשָׁר הֶעֱוֵיתִי וְלֹא שָׁוָה לִי: (כח) פָּדָה נפשי מֵעֲבֹר בַּשָּׁחַת וחיתי בָּאוֹר תִּרְאֶה: (כט) הֶן כָּל אֵלֶּה יִפְעַל אֵל פַּעֲמַיִם שָׁלוֹשׁ עִם גָּבֶר: (ל) לְהָשִׁיב נַפְשׁוֹ מִנִּי שָׁחַת לֵאוֹר בְּאוֹר הַחַיִּים: (לא) הַקְשֵׁב אִיּוֹב שְׁמַע לִי הַחֲרֵשׁ וְאָנֹכִי אֲדַבֵּר: (לב) אִם יֵשׁ מִלִּין הֲשִׁיבֵנִי דַּבֵּר כִּי חָפַצְתִּי צַדְּקֶךָּ: (לג) אִם אַיִן אַתָּה שְׁמַע לִי הַחֲרֵשׁ וַאֲאַלֶּפְךָ חָכְמָה: ס

ב. רד"ק תהלים קאפיטל קז פסוק א

(א) הֹדוּ לַה'. המזמור הזה נאמר על ארבעה שיצאו מצרה לרווחה, וצריכים להודות לה', כי הוא המוציאם מצרה לרווחה. ואינו בדרך מקרה כאשר יחשבו [חכמי המחקר] התועים [שיאמרו האדם תחת המזל, ואין אנו מאמינים בהשם]. אלא צריכים שיודו, כי בעבור עונש עונם היו בצרה ובחסד אלהים ניצלו מהצרה בצעקתם לו. וכן למדו רז"ל מזה המזמור ואמרו [ברכות נד, ב]: ארבעה צריכין להודות ולברך האל יתברך ברבים. והם הנזכרים במזמור הזה, הולכי מדברות, ומי שהיה חבוש בבית האסורים ויצא, ומי שהיה חולה ונתרפא, ויורדי הים. וזכר גם כן בזה המזמור מי שהם בטוב במקומם, יביאם האל יתברך לחסרון הטוב והיותם ברע. ומי שהם ברע במקומם, ישגבם האל ויושיעם מרעתם, ויתן להם טובה גדולה. כל זה להורות כי הכל הוא מיד האל, הרע והטוב:

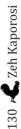

ג. תשובות הגאונים - שערי תשובה סימן רצט

מר רב ששנא גאון ז"ל וששאלתם האי שאנו רגילים לשחוט ערב
יוה"כ תרנגולים ואין אנו יודעים מנהג זה למה אי משום תמורה מאי
שנא תרנגול מבהמה וחיה הא ודאי קושיא היא. וי"ל שיש בה שני
טעמים אחד שתרנגול מצוי בביתו של אדם מבהמה וחיה ועוד יש
במקומנו עשירים שעושים תמורה אילים ועיקר מבעלי קרנים דמות
אילו של יצחק אבינו לפיכך לא דבר קבוע הוא. ועוד שמענו מחכמים
ראשונים שאף על פי שיש מי שעושה תמורה בבהמה שדמיה יקרים
תרנגול מובחר לפי ששמו גבר כדאמרי' מאי קריאת הגבר. אמר רב
קרא גברא דבי רב שילא אמרי קרא תרנגולא. ותניא כותיה דר' שילא
היוצא קודם קריאת הגבר דמו בראשו וכיון ששמו גבר תמורת גבר
וטפי מהני ומעלי.

וכך צריך אוחז שליח תרנגול ומניח ידו על ראש התרנגול ונוטלו
מניחו על ראש מתכפר ואומר זה תחת זה וזה חילוף זה זה מחול
על זה ומחזירו עליו פעם אחת ואומרי' יושבי חשך וצלמות כו'
ויוציאם מחשך וצלמות כו' אוילים מדרך פשעם כו' כל אוכל
תתעב נפשם וגו' ויצעקו אל ה' בצר להם וגו' ישלח דברו וירפאם
יודו לה' חסדו וגו' ויחננו ויאמר פדעהו וגו' נפש תחת נפש.
ועושה כסדר הזה ז' פעמים ואחר כן מניח ידו על ראש תרנגול
ואומר זה יצא למיתה תחת זה ומניח ידו על ראש מתכפר ואומר
תכנס אתה פלוני בן פלוני לחיים ולא תמות ועושה כסדר הזה ג'
פעמים ומניח מתכפר ידו על ראש תרנגול תבנית סמיכה וסומך
ידו עליו ושוחטו לאלתר. תבנית תכף לסמיכה שחיטה:

ד. תשובות הגאונים החדשות - עמנואל (אופק)
סימן י

תשלא. וששאלתם שאנו רגילין לשחוט ערב יום הכיפורים תרנגול
מה קורין עליו. רגילין כאן אוחז שליח צבור תרנגול ומניח ידו על
ראש התרנגול ומניחה על ראש המתכפר ואומר זה תחת זה,
זה חליפי זה, זה תמורת זה, זה מחול על זה, ומחזירו על ראש
המתכפר שניה ואומרים שלשה בני אדם מזמור ק"ז (תהלים קז)
הודו לה' וגו', יאמרו גאולי ה' וגו' כלו עד ויתבוננו חסדי ה', זה תחת
זה וכו' שלשה פעמים, זה למיתה תחת זה ולא תמות, הכנס אתה
פלוני בן פלוניתא לחיים תחת זה ולא תמות ג' פעמים, ומניח

מתכפר ידו על ראש התרנגול תבנית סמיכה וישחוט לאלתר
כדאמרי' (ברכות מב, א) תכף לסמיכה שחיטה. ואף על פי שיש
לעשות תמורה בבהמה גסה שדמיהם יקרים יותר מתרנגול, אף
על פי כן תרנגול מובחר מפני ששמו גבר תמורת גבר כדאמרינן
(יומא כ, ב) מאי קריאת הגבר, רב אמר קרא גברא דבי ר' שילא
אמרי קרא תרנגולתא, תניא (יומא כא, א) כותיה דר' שילא היוצא
קודם קריאת הגבר דמו בראשו.

ה. תשובות הגאונים - מוסאפיה (ליק) סימן ח

לרב האיי. וששאלתם שאנו רגילים ליקח ראשים של כבשים בר"ה
לאכול ולשחוט כל א' תרנגול בערב יום הכפורים. וכו', ושאלתם
לפרש לכם. זה נחש הוא לטובה לחכמים ורוב אנשי בבל רגילין
לעשות.

בערב ר"ה לוקחין בשר או ראשים ומבשלין אותו בטסני או בדבר
של מתיקה ואין מבשלין בישול שיש בו חומץ. ואומרים כך נאכל מיני
מתיקה כל השנה. ובשר שמן כדי שתהא שנה כלה מתוקה וערבה
ולא יהיה בה דבר רע ודבר צרה.

ו. רש"י מסכת שבת דף פא עמוד ב

האי פרפיסא - עציץ נקוב שזרעו בו, ובתשובת הגאונים מצאתי:
שעושין חותלות מכפות תמרים, וממלאין אותם עפר וזבל בהמה,
ועשרים ושנים או חמישה עשר יום לפני ראש השנה עושין כל אחד
ואחד לשם כל קטן וקטנה שבבית, וזורעים לתוכן פול המצרי או
קיטנית, וקורין לו פורפיסא, וצומח, ובערב ראש השנה נוטל כל אחד
שלו, ומחזירם סביבות ראשו שבעה פעמים, ואומר: זה תחת זה, וזה
חליפתי וזה תמורתי, ומשליכו לנהר.

ז. שו"ת הרשב"א חלק א סימן שצה

מונטפשליר. לחכם רבי יעקב בר מכיר. כתב מר כי ראית מה
שהשבתי אני בענין הכפרה שעושין לנערים בערבי יום הכפורים
שאסרתי אני. והנאך ואתה מוסיף עוד לומר שקרוב לומר
שהשחיטה פסולה שזה כמו שוחט לשם חטאת. אני מצאתי מנהג
זה פשוט בעירנו עם שאר דברים שהיו נוהגין כיוצא בזה. שהיו

שוחטין תרנגול זקן לכפרה על הנער היולד וחותכים ראשו ותולים הראש בנוצתו בפתח הבית עם שומים. והבלי' הרבה שנראו בעיני כדרכי האמורי ודחקתי על זה הרבה. ובחסד עליון נשמעו דברי ולא נשאר מכל זה ומכיוצא באלו בעירנו מאומה. אף על פי ששמעתי מפי אנשים הגונים מאד מאשכנז היושבים עמנו בבית המדרש שכל רבני ארצם עושין כן ערבי יום הכפורים ושוחטין לכפרה אווזין ותרנגולין. גם שמעתי כי נשאל לרבינו האיי גאון ז"ל ואמר שכן נהגו. ועם כל זה מנעתי המנהג הזה מעירנו. ומכל מקום אינו רואה לפיסול השחיטה מפני שלא פסלו אלא השוחט לשם דבר הנדר והנדב. ודוקא תמימים אבל בעלי מומין לא. לפי שכל הרואה יודע שאין זה לשם עולה ולשם שלמים דוקא אלא דברי הבאי בעלמא. ולפיכך כתבתי אני בספרי ספר תורת הבית שהשוחט תרנגולין אווזין לשם מכל אלו ששחיטתן כשרה. לפי שהכל יודעין שאין אחד מאלו עולין לקרבן.

ח.   רדב"ז ח"ב סי' שמ"ה

ועל ענין שחיטת התרנגולים ערב יום הכפורים לכפרה על הנערים העולם נהגו בו היתר, אבל הרשב"א אסר. ומסתברא לי שאם נותנין התרנגולים לעניים שאפילו הרב מודה שאין בזה משום דרכי האמורי, ודמיא להא דתניא (ראש השנה ד' א') סלע זה לצדקה כדי שיחיה בני וכו', ולא ראיתי בכל חכמי הדור מי שמיחה בדבר.

ט.   טור אורח חיים הלכות יום הכפורים סימן תרה

יש מקומות שנוהגין לשחוט תרנגול לכפרה, וכן יש בתשובת הגאונים, וששאלתם שאנו נוהגין לשחוט ערב יום הכפורים תרנגול ואין אנו יודעין מנהג זה למה אי משום תמורה מאי שנא תרנגול מבהמה חיה, הא ודאי קושיא הוא אלא שיש בה טעמים אחד שהתרנגול מצוי בבית יותר מכל בהמה חיה ועוף, ועוד יש במקומות עשירים עושין תמורת אילים ועיקר בעלי קרנים דמות אילו של יצחק אבינו לפיכך לא דבר קבוע הוא. ועוד שמענו מחכמים הראשונים שאף על פי שבהמה דמיה יקרים יותר מתרנגול אף על פי כן תרנגול מובחר לפי ששמו גבר, כדאמרינן (ביומא כ א) מאי קרא גברא אמר רב שילא קרא תרנגולא, וכיון ששמו גבר תמורת גבר בגבר מהני ומעלי.

וכך רגילין כאן אוחז ש"צ התרנגול ומניח ידו על ראשו ונוטלו ומניח על ראש המתכפר ואומר זה תחת זה זה חילוף זה זה מחולל על זה ומחזירו עליו פעם אחת ואומר (תהלים ק"ז) יושבי חשך וצלמות אסירי עני וברזל יוציאם מחשך וצלמות ומוסרותיהם ינתק אוילים מדרך פשעם ומעונותיהם יתענו ויצעקו אל ה' בצר להם ממצוקותיהם' יושיעם ישלח דברו וירפאם וימלט משחיתותם ידו לה' חסדו ונפלאותיו לבני אדם תחת נפש. ועושה כסדר הזה ג' פעמים, ואחר כך מניח ידו על ראש התרנגול תבנית סמיכה וסומך עליו ושוחטו לאלתר תיכף לסמיכה שחיטה.

ורגילין לתתו לעניים כדי שיהא כפרה לנפשו. ומה שרגילין לזרוק את בני מעיו על הגג כדי ליתנם לעופות, יש להביא קצת ראיה מההיא דמסכת חולין רמי בר תמרי איקלע למערבא מעלי יומא דכפורי חזא דקא שדו כבדא וכולייא אזיל שקלינהו משום דהאידנא דהיתרא שכיח טפי:

י.   בית יוסף אורח חיים סימן תרה

אם נכון למנוע מעשה הכפרה שעושים לנערים בערב יום הכפורים:

יש מקומות שנוהגים לשחוט תרנגול לכפרה וכן יש בתשובת הגאונים. המרדכי במסכת יומא (סי' תשכג) כתב המנהג הזה וכל מה שכתוב בסימן זה הוא בפסקי הרא"ש למסכת יומא (פ"ח סי' כג) וקצתו במרדכי (שם וסי' תשכז) ומנהג זה כתוב גם בתשב"ץ (תשב"ץ קטן סי' קכה) וכתוב שם שנוהגים ליקח תרנגול לזכר ותרנגולת לנקיבה:

והרשב"א כתב בתשובה (ח"א סי' שצה) בענין הכפרה שעושין לנערים בערב יום הכפורים מנהג זה פשוט בעירנו ואף על פי ששמעתי מפי אנשים הגונים מאשכנז שכל רבני ארצם עושים כן וגם שמעתי שנשאל רבינו האיי ואמר שכן נהגו עם כל זה מנעתי המנהג הזה מעירנו וכתוב בארחות חיים (הל' ערב יוה"כ אות א) שהרמב"ן אוסרו משום דרכי האמורי:

יא.   שולחן ערוך הלכות יום הכפורים

סימן תר"ה סעיף א'

מה שנוהגים לעשות כפרה בערב יום כיפורים לשחוט תרנגול על כל בן זכר ולומר עליו פסוקים, יש למנוע המנהג.

הגה: ויש מהגאונים שכתבו מנהג זה, וכן כתבו אותו רבים מן האחרונים, וכן נוהגין בכל מדינות אלו, ואין לשנות, כי הוא מנהג ותיקין.

ונוהגין ליקח תרנגול זכר לזכר, ולנקבה לוקחין תרנגולת (ב"י בשם תשב"ץ), ולוקחין למעוברת שני תרנגולים אולי תלד זכר.

ובוחרין בתרנגולים לבנים, על דרך שנאמר אם יהיו חטאיכם כשנים כשלג ילבינו (ישעיה א, יח).

ונהגו ליתן הכפרות לעניים, או לפדותן במממן שנותנים לעניים (מהרי"ל).

וכו'. ויש להסמיך שחיטת הכפרות מיד לאחר שהחזירו עליו וסמך ידיו עליו, דמות הקרבן.

וזורקין בני מעיהם על הגגות או בחצר, מקום שהעופות יכולין לקחת משם (טור).

יב.   מגן אברהם סימן תרה

א ויש מהגאונים - וכן כתב האר"י בכוונות על פי הקבלה, ושל"ה. האר"י שחטו באשמור' אחר הסליחות כי אז רחמים גוברים (של"ה):

ב שני תרנגולים - כלומר תרנגול ותרנגולת אף אם העובר נקבה די לה ולבתה באחת משום ששנים רשאים ליקח כפרה אחת (לבוש) וכן נוהגים אפילו בשני גופים וכן משמע סוף פרק י"ב דמנחות, והאר"י לקח ג' (של"ה):

ג בתרנגולים לבנים - מכל מקום אין לחזור אחר לבנים דוקא דהוה כעין דרכי האמורי כדאיתא בפרק קמא דעבודה זרה, אלא אם יזדמן לו לבן יקח (ב"ח). ואם אין לו תרנגול יקח שאר בעל חי, ויש אומרים אפילו דגים (לבוש). ונראה לי דלא יקח דבר הראוי להקרבה כגון תורים ובני יונה שלא יהא נראה כמקדיש קדשים בחוץ, עיין בטור. ואיתא בשבת דף פ"א ע"ב ברש"י שהיו נוהגים ליקח עציץ עם הזרעים ולהחזירו סביב ראשו (בע"ה) (בערב ראש השנה). יאמר חליפתי תמורתי כפרתי ר"ת חת"ך שם מלאך (ד"מ הגמ"נ):

ד או לפדותו כו' - וזה טוב יותר כדי שלא יתביישו העניים (של"ה ומהרי"ל):

יג.   משנה ברורה סימן תרה

(א) יש למנוע המנהג - משום חמש דרכי האמורי:

(ב) מנהג ותיקין - ויחשוב [ב] שכל מה שעושין לעוף הזה הכל היה ראוי לבוא עליו ועל ידי תשובתו הקדוש ברוך הוא מסלק הגזירה מעליו ונתקיים דוגמתו בעוף הזה וכן כתבו הראשונים טעם הקרבן הבא על השוגג.

וטוב לשחטו באשמורת אחר הסליחות כי אז הרחמים גוברים. ולכן יש לבעל הבית להזמין אבוקה לפי שאין שוחטין בלילה כי אם לאור האבוקה. ויש ששוחטין אותו אחר תפלת שחרית [עיין א"ר].

ובמקום שמתקבצים הרבה ביחד ודוחקין זה את זה והשוחטים נעורים כל הלילה בפנים זעופים ואינם מרגישים בסכין מפני רוב העבודה, ויוכל לבוא לידי איסור נבילה, טוב יותר לשחוט הכפרות יום או יומים קודם יוה"כ כי כל עשרת ימי תשובה הוא זמן לכפרות [פמ"ג ע"ש]. או שיסבבו על ראשיהם במעות ותחשב להם לצדקה שלא יהיו נכשלין באיסור נבילה ח"ו.

[ומי שיכול ורוצה מן המובחר יקרא השוחט לביתו באשמורת הבוקר. וכהיום המנהג בכמה מקומות שהשוחטין נעורים והולכין לבית כל אחד אחר חצות הלילה עד אור היום, ולכן מן הנכון שישנו השוחטים מקודם כדי שלא יתעלפו. וכן צריכים להכין כמה סכינים בדוקים ובשעת שחיטה יראה לבדוק בכל פעם ולא יסמוך על מה שבדק תחילה.

והנה אף כשישוחט בבית בעה"ב הדרך הוא שבאים גם כן מבעלי בתים הסמוכים ובפרט כשישוחט בביתו באים הרבה שלוחים ביחד עם כפרות, ומחמת שצריך לשחוט הרבה כפרות אין הזמן מספיק לבדוק בכוונת הלב כדין י"ב בדיקות, וקרוב הדבר שמחמת הנחיצה לא ידקדק היטב בבדיקה, לכן העצה היעוצה שעל כל פנים אחר שחיטת כל העופות של בעל הבית אחד יבדוק טרם ילך השליח עם העופות כדי שיתברר לו אם נמצא סכינו יפה, שאסור לאכול קודם הבירור ואם נמצא פגום יטרוף כל העופות של בעל הבית זה]:

(ג) ב' תרנגולים - דהיינו תרנגול ותרנגולת, תרנגול שמא הולד זכר, ותרנגולת שאפילו אם הולד נקבה יתכפרו שניהם היא עצמה

טו. ספר שבולי הלקט סדר ראש השנה סימן רפג

מצאתי בתשובת הגאונים זצ״ל וששאלתם לפרש לכם למה רגילין לאכול ראשי כבשים בראש השנה ולאכול ולשחוט כל אחד ואחד תרנגול בערב יום הכיפורים. חכמים וכל אנשי בבל כך עושין. בערב ראש השנה לוקחין בשר שמן או ראשו של צאן ומבשלין אותה בטיסני או בדבר של מתיקה ואין מבשלין בישול שיש בו חומץ כל עיקר ואומרים נאכל מתיקה ובישול שמן כדי שתהא כל השנה מתוקה וטובה ועריבה עלינו ולא יהיה דבר רע. ובערב ראש השנה שוחטין כל אחד ואחד שבבית תרנגול ומחזירין אותן בחייהן על כל אחד ואחד ואומר זה תחת זה חילוף זה יצא זה למיתה ויכנס זה פלוני בן פלוני לחיים ושוחטין אותו ומשגרין אותן ליתומים ולעניים ואומר יהי כופר נפשנו ויהא כפרה עלינו. וחכמים ובעלי בתים אף בערב יום הכיפורים עושין כן. ויש מחזירין אילים וכבשים. וכל זה נחש לטובה היא במסכת כריתות פרק קמא אמר אביי השתא דאמרת סימנא מילתא היא יהא רגיל למיחזי אינש בריש שתא קרא רוביא כרתי וסילקא ותמרי. פי' קרא דלעת על שם דלו עיני למרום רוביא על שם פרו ורבו ופירש רבינו שלמה זצ״ל תלתן פונוגרוקי בלע״ז כרתי יכרתו איבינו והן כרישין סילקא יסולקו עונותינו תמרי תמו עונותינו:

טז. מאירי - חבור התשובה (משיב נפש, מאמר ב' פרק ח')

ומנהג אחר נהגו זקנים ביום זה שהוא צריך לעיין עליו והוא שהתינוקות מביאין לפניהם תרנגולים ושוחטים אותם וקוראין עליהם פסוקים, כמעט שמחללין קדושת התינוק על התרנגול, כאלו היה התינוק הקדש או מעשר שני שירצו לחלל קדשתו על התרנגול ומחליפין וממירין זה תחת זה, עד שמתגלגלין ובאין להיות תכלית היוצא מדבריהם שיהא תרנגול זה פורש למיתה והלה פורש לחיים.

ונתפשט מנהג זה באמתנו עד שהוקבע בסדור המחזורים כנוסח ודוי של יום הכפורים עצמו מבלי שנדע לדבר זה שורש או יסוד בתלמוד כלל. ולא עוד אלא שכשלו בו רבים לעשות כן מדרך נחש וסימן עד שכבר מחו קצת גאונים במנהג זה, וחלקו הרבה במעשה ולא נענו,

---

והולד באחת. ואפילו שני בני אדם יכולין ליקח כפרה אחת אם אין ידם משגת. ויש שלוקחין למעוברת שני תרנגולות ותרנגול אחד.

ובשעה שמסבב על ראשו יאמר זה חליפתי תמורתי כפרתי ר״ת חת״ך, שם מלאך הממונה על החיים:

(ד) בתרנגולים לבנים - ומ״מ אין לחזור אחרי לבנים דוקא כמו שנוהגין אנשים שמהדרין אחריהם ביותר ונותנין ביוקר והוא מדרכי האמורי וחוק עכו״ם אלא אם יבא ממילא לקנות במקח שאר תרנגולים יקנה אותו ולא יאמר כלום [אחרונים]. כתבו האחרונים אם אין לו תרנגול יקח אווז או שאר בעלי חיים שאינם ראוים להקרבה למזבח וי״א אפילו דגים:

(ה) ונהגו ליתן - כמש״כ וחטאיך בצדקה פרוק וכו' ובאמת לפדותו טוב יותר שלא יתביישו העניים שיאמר זה נתן עוונותיו על ראשו ושלחו אלי ואם יודע בו שלא יתבייש יכול ליתן לו העופות עצמם שלפעמים נהנה יותר שהוא הנאה שא״צ לטרוח:

(ו) בממון שנותנין וכו' - ר״ל שיעריך דמי שיווי הכפרות ששחטן ויחלק דמי השיווי לעניים והיינו אם היכולת בידו. וכתבו האחרונים דמי שפודה אותו ויש בידו מעות מעשר שלו לא יפדה בהם רק במעות של חולין:

(ז) על הקברות ולהרבות - ויוכל ליתן זה ממעות פדיון הכפרות...:

(ח) וסמך ידיו עליו - ויש שכתבו שיש למנוע דבר זה דנראה כמקדיש קדשים ושוחטן בחוץ ואחרים כתבו שאין לחוש לזה כיון שהתרנגול אינו ראוי למזבח:

(ט) וזורקין - שדרך התרנגולים ליזון מן הגזל ובני המעיים הם הכלים הראשונים שמקבלים הגזל לכן מרחיקין עצמם מלאכלם כדי ליתן אל לבו להרחיק מן הגזל וגם משום רחמניות כשם שמרחם על הבריות לפרנסן ירחמו עליו מן השמים:

יד. שער הציון סימן תרה

(ב) במשנה ברורה ס״ק (ב) מנהג ותיקין - וחישוב שכל מה שעושין כדוגמא ד' מיתות בית דין, שזרקו לעוף אחר שחיטה הוא כעין סקילה, ומה שהשוחט תופסו בצואר ושוחטו ומחרכין אותו באש הוא דוגמא שרפה והרג וחנק [מהרי״ן]:

מפני שסמכו רוב הגאונים להיות עולם כמנהגא נוהג בענין זה, כענין מה שאמרו (הוריות י"ב א') בענין קרכס"ת [קרא, רוביא, כרתי, סלקא, תמרי] "השתא דאמרת סימנא מילתא היא ליחזי איניש בריש שתא קרכס"ת," וכמו שבארנו במקומו.

ולדעתי רצו לומר בזה, שאין הכונה במנהג רק להעיר לב האדם ולהרעידו להיות מראה את עצמו כאלו הוא ובני ביתו מחויבים לשם מצד עונותיו, ושאם ישוב לשם בכל לבו יהפך השם אליו את הקללה לברכה ויקרע גזר דינו בתכלית תשובתו. והוא שהיה מכלל המנהג היותם סמוך לזה מרבים בצדקה לשלוח מנות לאביונים עם התרנגולים ההם איש כמתנת ידו. ועל זה הצד תקנו בו לפי דעתי פסוקים יורו על זה ויצעקו אל יי בצר להם וממצוקותיהם יצילם ישלח דברו וירפאם וגו' ויחנה ויאמר פדעהו" וגו', ופסוקים אחרים יורו על דמיון זאת התכונה. והיתה כונתם בקריאת הפסוקים האלו שלא יטעו לדמות היות הענין דרך נחש חלילה כמו שכתבתי בענין קרבס"ת.

ומצאתי בדברי הגאונים ענין דומה לוה יורה גם כן היות עיקר המנהג לזכור ולהיות החי נותן אל לבו ענינים יביאוהו לידי יראת השם. והוא שכתבו הגאונים שעיקר מנהג זה באיל בעל קרנים, אלא שאחר כן נתפשט המנהג כתרנגולים, אם מצד המצאו בבית מזומנת, אם מצד היותו נקרא גבר בלשון חכמים כאמרם (יומא כ' ב') ז"ל מאי קריאת הגבר ר' שילא אמר קרא התרנגול. והיה נאות אצלם בהערת התמורה נפש בנפש בשתוף השם. אבל עקר המנהג היה באיל על שם שאירע ליצחק אבינו שהיה רצון השם להצילו ולהעמיד איל תחתיו, יזכרו בזה ענין העקדה שאנו מכונים בה לזכרה תמיד באלו הימים כמו שכתבנו. עד שנתעורר בזכירתה גבול אהבת השם ויראתו עד היכן מגעת, כמו שכבר קדם לנו.

וכמדומה באלו הדרכים ראוי להבין במחזיקים במנהג, ומי יתן והיה לבבם זה לראות את השם הנכבד והנורא ולקחת המנהגים בדרך הנאות והמבוקש, לא דרך בלתי מכוון ולא מצוה מלומדה כמו שבארנו הטבילה וכו'.

יז.   ספר מהרי"ל (מנהגים) הלכות ערב יום כיפור

[ב] מהרא"ק: בערב יו"כ כשאוחז התרנגול בידו להתכפר בו נכון לומר זה 'חליפתי, העולם נוהגין כמו סדר מהרא"ק על עצמו זה

חליפתי כו', ועל אחר זה חליפתך וכו', ועל אשה זה חליפתך וכו' ואומרי' פסוקים כאשר בא"ח. זה 'תחתי, זה 'תמורתי, זה 'כפרתי. לפי שר"ת שלו חת"ך, והוא שמו של מלאך הממונה על זה ויוצא מפסוק באשרי פותח' את' ידך' (תהלים קמה, טז), ס"ת חת"ך, והוא השם הנז' בהאוחז החות"ך חיים לכל חי. וז"ל א"ח: כך רגילין שליח אוחז תרנגול ומחזירו על ראשו ונוטלו ומניחו על ראש המתכפר ואומר: זה תחת זה, זה חילוף זה, זה מחול על זה, ומחזירו עליו פעם אחת ואומר: בני אדם יושבי חשך וצלמות אסירי עני וברזל, יוציאם מחשך וצלמות ומוסרותיהם ינתק, אוילים מדרך פשעם ומעונותיהם יתענו, ויזעקו אל ה' בצר להם ממצוקותיהם יושיעם, ישלח דבריו וירפאם וימלט משחיתותם, יודו לה' חסדו ונפלאותיו לבני אדם, נפש תחת נפש.

כל אלו מלקוטי פסוקי דבספר תהלים מזמור סימן ק"ז, ורובא דעלמא מוסיפין לומר גם פסוק זה מספר איוב (לג, כג - ד) וז"ל, אם יש עליו מלאך מליץ אחד מני אלף להגיד לאדם ישרו ויחננו ויאמר פדעהו מרדת שחת מצאתי כופר.

ועושה כסדר הזה ג"פ. ואח"כ מניח ידו על ראש התרנגול תבנית סמיכה וסומך עליו ושוחטו לאלתר תיכף לסמיכה שחיטה. אמר מהר"י סג"ל אשה מעוברת תקח שתי כפרות והאחד בשביל העובר.

מהר"י סג"ל נהג ליטול תרנגול לבן לכפרה דחטאים אדומים הם, ויתקיים ביה אם יאדימו כתולע כצמר יהיו (ישעיה א, יח). דרש מהר"י סג"ל יש מקומות שנותנים הכפרות גופן לעניים, והוכשר מנהג ריינוס שנותנים מעות שוים לעניים דאז לא מתבייש העני מלקבלם. אבל כשנותנים את התרנגול גופו' אומר העני זה השליך עונותיו על תרנגול זה ונבזה אני לו ששלחו אלי.

יח.   שו"ת מהר"י ווייל סימן קצא

הג"ה במיימוני", בערב יום כפורים יעשה כפרות ויאמר חת"ך ר"ת חליפתי תמורתי כפרתי, זהו שם החותך חיים לכל חי. ויחשוב בלבו שהוא חייב מיתה כמו זה. והיינו טעם הקרבנות. זורקו לארץ כעין סקילה, שוחטו הרג, תופסו בידו בצואר הבהמה היינו חנק, שורפו היינו שריפה. היינו דכתיב מצרה נחלץ צדיק ויבא רשע רשע תחתיו

וכתוב פדעהו מרדת שחת מצאתי כופר, כיון שיצא המשחית אינו משיב אלא אם כן צריך לחול על שום דבר, והיינו טעמא דעגלה ערופה.

יט. מהר"ל, נתיב הבטחון פרק א'

עוד שם, אמר רב הונא אמר רב משום ר' מאיר וכן תנא משמיה דר' עקיבא לעולם יהא אדם רגיל לומר כל דעבדין מן שמיא לטב, כי הא דר' עקיבא הוי אזיל באורחא והוי בהדיה חמרא ותרנגולא ושרגא מטא להאי דוכתא בעי אושפיזא ולא יהבו ליה, אמר כל דעבדין מן שמיא לטב, אזל בת בדברא אתא אריה אכליה לחמריה אתא שונרא אכליה לתרנגולא אתא זיקא כבי לשרגא, אמר כל דעבדין מן שמיא לטב עביד. בלילא אתא גייסא שבייה למתא, אמר להן היינו דאמרי כל דעבדין מן שמיא לטב עביד, כבר אמרנו בנתיב האהבה כי אלו ג' דברים הם ג' חלקי האדם שהם הגוף והנפש והשכל, הגוף החמרי הוא מתיחס לחמור ועליו רוכב הנפש, והנפש מתיחס אל התרנגול שנקרא גבר ואיש וידוע כי הנפש הוא צורה אשר הצורה נקרא איש כמו שידוע והחומר נקרא אשה כמו שהתבאר פעמים הרבה, ולכך אמר שהיה לו חמרא ותרנגולא, והשלישי הוא הנר שהוא כנגד השכל שנקרא נר שהוא המאיר לאדם ובכל מקום נקרא השכל נר וכמו שאמרו במס' שבת בפ' במה מדליקין (כ"ג ב') הזהיר בנר הויין לו בנים תלמידי חכמים שנאמר כי נר מצוה ותורה אור.

ודבר פשוט שהשכל הוא הנר המאיר לאדם ואין צריך ביאור דבר זה, ומפני שכשבא ר"ע לאותה עיר היה ראוי לבא עליו גם כן מה שבא על כל העיר דהיינו שיהיה נשבה כמו שהיו נשבים שאר העיר ואם היה נשבה היו מבטלים אותו מכל והיו נוטלים ממנו גופו ונפשו וגם שכל שלו שהיו מבטלים אותו לגמרי, והשם יתברך רצה להציל את רבי עקיבא סבב דלא יהבי ליה אושפיזא, וכאשר היה בעיר היה בכלל אותה גזירה להיות נשבה, ואי אפשר שלא יהיה הגזירה שיצאת על העיר ג"כ שולט בו ואינו אפשר שלא יעשה זה בו רושם של דבר מה. ולפיכך אתא אריה ואכל החמור ובא השונרא ואכיל התרנגול ודבר זה הוא תמורת נפשו וכפרתו, והנר שכבה הוא תמורת השכל עד שהיה לו תמורה לגמרי.

ומזה ראיה גמורה מן הגמרא ליקח תרנגול לכפרה על נפשו בערב יום הכפורים, ודבר זה ידוע.

ולפיכך אמר ר' עקיבא כל מה דעביד רחמנא כלומר כי הוא בוטח בה' כי מה שנעשה לו לטב עביד ומחמת בטחונו בו יתברך נעשה לו הדבר ההוא לטובה מדבר שהיה נראה רע.

כ. לבוש אורח חיים סימן תרה

לכך לוקחים מינים הללו שידעו הכל שלא לשם קרבן הנהיגוהו אלא כדי להשביע עינו של רשע, הוא יצר הרע הוא שטן הוא מלאך המות, החפץ בהשחתת העולם ומקטרג על הבריות כדי שימסרו בידו, וכשישחט כל אחד מין בעל חי במקומו, ויחשוב כאילו שחט את עצמו אין לו מקום לקטרג כל כך, ועל דרך שעיר המשתלח לעזאזל, כן נ"ל לקיים המנהג.

כא. פני יהושע בבא קמא דף נ עמוד א

תנו רבנן, מעשה בבתו של נחוניא חופר שיחין שנפלה לבור גדול, באו והודיעו את רבי חנינא בן דוסא. שעה ראשונה (שעדיין היא ראויה להיות חיה בתוך המים) אמר להם שלום (תעלה וכן שניה), שניה אמר להם שלום, שלישית (דהוה לה שהות שתצא נפשה אם ישנה שם) אמר להם עלתה (כבר עלתה ודאי כדאמרין לקמן דפשיטא ליה דלא תמות שם).

אמרו לה מי העלך, אמרה להם זכר (אילו של יצחק) של רחלים נזדמן לי וזקן אחד (אברהם) מנהיגו. אמרו לו נביא אתה, אמר להם לא נביא אנכי ולא בן נביא אנכי, אלא כך אמרתי דבר שאותו צדיק מצטער בו (לחפור בורות ומערות לעולי רגלים) יכשל בו זרעו.

בגמרא אמרו לה מי העלך אמרה להו זכר של רחלים וזקן אחד מנהיגו ופרש"י איל של אברהם. ויראה שרמזה בזה דודאי נגזר עליה משמים למיתה, אלא שהועיל לה תפילתו של רבי חנינא בן דוסא, וכיון שנגזר עליה משמים אי אפשר לבטל הגזירה עד שיותן תמורתה איזה אדם אחר, כדמצינו בכמה דוכתא, בנחל קישון (פסחים קי"ח ע"ב) וכעובדא דר' ביבי בחגיגה (דף ד' ע"ב), ועיקרו מפורש בזוהר גבי נחשא'. שלכך נוהגין העולם ליקח תרנגול בערב יו"כ לכפרה. ואם כן נרמז בזה העניין כמו שהיה באיל של יצחק שנקרב תמורתו כן נעשה לה וק"ל.

ובזה נתיישב מה שלא אמרו תיכף לרבי חנינא בן דוסא וכי נביא אתה אלא לאחר שאמרה זכר של רחלים, והיינו דעיקר תמיהתם כיון שאמרה שודאי נגזר עליה משמים למיתה אלא שתפלתו גרמה לה, על זה אמרו וכי נביא אתה פירוש איך כל כך בתפילתך, ועל זה השיב להם אמרתי דבר שנצטער וכו' על זה תמכתי יתדותי שתועיל תפילתי לבטל הגזירה, וק"ל:

כב.   חתם סופר מסכת שבת דף פא עמוד ב

המנהג אשכנז לעשות כפרות כמבואר בשולחן ערוך. ועיין מגן אברהם סי' תר"ה סוף סק"ג שמרמז על מה שהובא ברש"י שבת דף פ"א ע"ב בשם הגאונים, ונ"ל שהיה כן עושים כן שאם נגזר חלילה כריתת זרעו יהיה זרע העציץ הזה במקום זרעו ומשום כן זורעים אותו על שם קטן וקטנה שבבית ולהיות אסכרה מיתת הקטנים רחמנא לישזבן. ואמרינן פ' אלו נערות (כתובות ל' ב') מי שנתחייב חנק או טובע בנהר או מת בסרוכי היינו אסכרא ר"ל על כן זורקו לנהר שהוא במקום אסכרא ובזה יכופר לו ולבניו ויחיו:

כג.   חיי אדם כלל קמג

סעיף ד

כבר נתפשט המנהג לעשות כפרות בערב יום הכפורים, דהיינו שלוקחין תרנגול זכר לזכר ותרנגולת לנקבה. ולמעוברת ב', דהיינו תרנגול שמא הולד זכר, ותרנגולת, דאפילו אם הולד נקבה יתכפרו שניהם היא והולד כא'. ואפילו שני בני אדם יכולים ליקח כפרה אחת. ויש לוקחים למעוברת שני תרנגולות ותרנגול אחד.

ואמנם אף שכמה גאונים כתבו מנהג זה, מכל מקום מה שנשרש בלב ההמון שכל כפרת יום הכפורים תולה בזה, וכמעט שכפרות ואכילת מצה נחשב להם למצוה אחת וסוברים שאין להם כפרה ביום הכפורים אם לא בתרנגול, ועל ידי זה באים לידי איסור נבלה חס וחלילה, שדוחקין זה את זה בקהלות גדולות והשוחטים ניעורים כל הלילה בפנים זעופים ואינם מרגישים בסכין.

ואני לדידי צייתי ואינם רוצים לבטל מנהג זה, טוב יותר היה להם לסבב על ראשיהם במעות, כמו שכבר נשרש בלב עמי הארץ שאם אי אפשר להם להשיג תרנגול, אזי מסבבין במעות, שבאמת כן מצינו

במנהג קדמונים שהיו מסבבים בזרעים (כמש"כ המ"א בשם רש"י בשבת פ"א), ותחשב להם לצדקה, ושלא יהיו נכשלים באיסור נבלה חס וחלילה. ומכל שכן לפי מנהג הנכון ליתן הכפרות לעניים או לפדותן וליתן המעות לעניים.

ומי שיכול ורוצה מן המובחר, אזי יקרא להשוחט לביתו באשמורת הבוקר, ויהיה תיכף לסמיכה שחיטה.

אבל לא יחשוב שזהו כפרתו, אלא יחשוב שכל מה שעושין לעוף הזה הכל היה ראוי לבא עליו (כענין הכוונה בקרבנות), והקב"ה ברחמיו עבור התשובה שעשה, היפך הגזירה ונתקיים דוגמתו בעוף הזה (כענין שכתב הרמב"ן ריש פרשת לך לך בענין הליכת אברהם*).

גם יזהרו שלא ידקדקו אחר כפרות לבנים. וכבר נתפשט בין הנשים שאין לוקחין אחרים רק דוקא לבנים ומהדרין אחריהם ונותנין ביוקר, והוא מדרכי האמורי וחוק לעבודה זרה, ולכן יזהרו בזה. אלא אם ממילא יבוא לידו לקנות כמקח שאר תרנגולים, יקנה אותו ולא יאמר כלום.

והמנהג לזרוק בני מעיהם, לפי שנזונים מן הגזל ובני המעיים הם הכלים הראשונים שמקבלים הגזל, לכן מרחיקין עצמם מלאכלם כדי ליתן אל לבו להרחיק עצמו מגזל (תר"ה):

כד.   * דברי הרמב"ן המובאים בחיי אדם הנ"ל

רמב"ן בראשית יב:ו

ויעבר אברם בארץ עד מקום שכם - אומר לך כלל תבין אותו בכל הפרשיות הבאות בענין אברהם יצחק ויעקב, והוא ענין גדול, הזכירוהו רבותינו בדרך קצרה, ואמרו (תנחומא ט) כל מה שאירע לאבות סימן לבנים, ולכן יאריכו הכתובים בספור המסעות וחפירת הבארות ושאר המקרים, ויחשוב החושב בהם כאלו הם דברים מיותרים אין בהם תועלת, וכולם באים ללמד על העתיד, כי כאשר יבוא המקרה לנביא משלשת האבות יתבונן ממנו הדבר הנגזר לבא לזרעו.

ודע כי כל גזירת עירין כאשר תצא מכח גזירה אל פועל דמיון, תהיה הגזרה מתקיימת על כל פנים. ולכן יעשו הנביאים מעשה בנבואות

כמאמר ירמיהו שצוה לברוך והיה ככלותך לקרוא את דברי הספר הזה תקשור עליו אבן והשלכתו אל תוך פרת ואמרת ככה תשקע בבל וגו' (ירמיה נא סג סד). וכן ענין אלישע בהניחו זרועו על הקשת (מ"ב יג טז - יז), ויאמר אלישע ירה ויור ויאמר חץ תשועה לה' וחץ תשועה בארם. ונאמר שם (פסוק יט) ויקצוף עליו איש האלהים ויאמר להכות חמש או שש פעמים אז הכית את ארם עד כלה ועתה שלש פעמים תכה את ארם:

ולפיכך החזיק הקדוש ברוך הוא את אברהם בארץ ועשה לו דמיונות בכל העתיד להעשות בזרעו, והבן זה.

כה. דברי הרמב"ן בענין הקרבנות

ויקרא קאפיטל א פסוק ט

הטעם שאומרים בהם, כי בעבור שמעשי בני אדם נגמרים במחשבה ובדבור ובמעשה, צוה השם כי כאשר יחטא יביא קרבן, יסמוך ידיו עליו כנגד המעשה, ויתודה בפיו כנגד הדבור, וישרוף באש הקרב והכליות שהם כלי המחשבה והתאוה, והכרעים כנגד ידיו ורגליו של אדם העושים כל מלאכתו, ויזרוק הדם על המזבח כנגד דמו בנפשו, כדי שיחשוב אדם בעשותו כל אלה כי חטא לאלהיו בגופו ובנפשו, וראוי לו שישפך דמו וישרף גופו לולא חסד הבורא שלקח ממנו תמורה וכפר הקרבן הזה שיהא דמו תחת דמו, נפש תחת נפש, וראשי אברי הקרבן כנגד ראשי אבריו, והמנות להחיות בהן מורי התורה שיתפללו עליו. וקרבן התמיד, בעבור שלא ינצלו הרבים מחטוא תמיד. ואלה דברים מתקבלים מושכים את הלב כדברי אגדה:

כו. דברי רבינו בחיי בענין הקרבנות

רבינו בחיי ויקרא א:ט

(ט) והקטיר הכהן את הכל המזבחה עולה אשה ריח ניחוח לה'. על דרך הפשט: טעם הקרבנות הכל לתועלת האדם, כי חפץ ה' יתעלה באדם שהוא מבחר המין ובשבילו נברא העולם, שיהיה כלו שכלי כמלאך ה' צבאות בלא חטא, והיה כי יחטא ואשם מצד היצר הרע הנטוע בו, ראוי לו שיתנחם ויכיר ויתבונן בפחיתות עצמו ובערך רוממות האדון יתעלה אשר המרה את פיו, ויתחייב ששים

אל לבו כי חטא לפניו בגופו ובנפשו, ומפני שכל פעולות האדם נכללות בשלשה דברים והם: המעשה והדבור והמחשבה, שהם שלשה חלקי החטא, על כן תחייב התורה את האדם להביא קרבן על חטאו ושיסמוך את ידיו עליו כנגד המעשה, ושיתודה בפיו כנגד הדבור, ושישרוף כלי העצה והמחשבה שהסכימו בחטא והם הקרב והכליות כנגד המחשבה, כדי שיתכפר בשלשה דברים אלו על שלשת חלקי החטא, וראוי לו שיזרק דמו של קרבן על גבי המזבח כנגד דמו, וכאשר יעשה כל הענינים האלה יחשוב בלבו כי הוא מתחייב מיתה בחטאו, וראוי להענש בארבע מיתות בית דין שהם סקילה שרפה הרג וחנק, כשהוא לוקח הבהמה ומשליכה ודוחף אותה לארץ הרי זה כענין סקילה, וכאלו מודה שהוא חייב סקילה, וכשישוחט אותה ותקף בשעת שחיטה בצוארה כדי שלא ישהה, הרי שעשה הרג וחנק כאלו מודה שהוא חייב הרג וחנק, וכשהוא שורפה כאלו מודה שהוא חייב שרפה.

ודומה לזה דרשו רז"ל (תנחומא שלח יד) בענין העקדה: (בראשית כב, יג) "ויעלהו לעולה תחת בנו", מהו "תחת בנו", אלא על כל עבודה שהיה עושה אברהם באיל היה מתפלל: יהי רצון מלפניך שתהיה עבודה זו חשובה כאלו היא עשויה בבני, כאלו הוא שחוט, כאלו דמו זרוק, כאלו הוא נשרף ונעשה דשן. וכיון שהחוטא ראוי שיהיה דמו נשפך כדם הקרבן, ושיהיה גופו נשרף כגוף הקרבן, והקב"ה לוקח קרבנו ממנו תמורתו וכופרו, הנה זה חסד גמור אשר גמלהו הש"י ברחמי וברוב חסדיו לקח נפש הבהמה תחת נפשו ושיתכפר בה. וטעם זה נכון ומתיישב על הלב,

כז. סידור עיון תפילה

היא מעניו נתחי כפרך מצרים (ישעיה מ"ג) דתרגימו יהבת חליפך, לא יתן לאלהים כפרו (תהלים מ"ט) דתרגמו פורקוניה, מצאתי כפר (א"ב ל"ג) תרגומו פורקנא, כפר לצדיק עשרו ותחת רשעים בוגד (משלי כ"א י"ח) מלת כפר ומלת תחת מתורגם שלחופיה וטעמו כשנגזר צרה על צדיק וישר, שנכשל בעון מה, אף שכבר נתן רשות למשחית, כשהוא שב, יבא הרשע תחתיו ותפול ההשחתה עליו ולשון זה מורגל ברבותינו באמרם: הבן כשמזכיר את אביו תוך י"ב חדש יאמר הריני כפרת משכבו, ופירש בעל הערוך הריני במקומו לסבול יסורי עונשו, וזהו המכוון גם כן בשם כפרה, שהעונש והפגע הנגזר על האדם יהיה עוף זה תחתיו, וכו'.

כח. כף החיים סי' תר"ה אות כט

שם בהגה. שנוהגין לילך על הקברות וכו'. והצדקה שנותנין שם הוא פדיון הכפרות כדי קשל"ה מסכת יומא, וא"כ ראוי לתת כפי ערך הכפרות שיש לו מ"א סק"ה, גר"ז או ה'.

והיינו בערך הכפרות ששוים עתה אחר השחיטה ולא כערך שהיו שוים קודם השחיטה שהיו ביוקר.

והיינו אם יש יכולת בידו לפדות וכן כתב המשנה ברורה שם וכ"מ ממ"ש לעיל או' ו' ועו"ש.

כט. כף החיים סי' תר"ה אות לד

אם אין מצוין שם עופות לקחת אותם אין צריך לזרקם.

ל. מכתב מאליהו יום כפור - תקמ"א

העושים כפרות על ממון לכאורה טועים שאין עיקר הכוונה כאן נתינת הצדקה אלא ציור המיתה שהרי אין אומרים עוף זה יהיה לצדקה אלא אומרים "ילך למיתה."

לא. דברי מנחם יום הכפורים סימן י"ח:

מנהג כפרות בערב יוהכ"פ:

השאלה על דבר מה שכתוב בשולחן ערוך (דפוס ראשון שלד) או"ח סי' תר"ה בהנושא של הסימן נדפס, מנהג כפרות בערב יום הכפורים מנהג של שטות. ובשאר הדפוסים נשמטו המילים "מנהג של שטות" ובפנים כתב המחבר יש למנוע המנהג, והלשון מנהג של שטות תמוה, אחרי שמביא בעצמו בבית יוסף שמקור המנהג נמצא בגאונים ושם נהגו.

תשובה מקור הדברים שיש לבטל המנהג הביא הבית יוסף שהוא בשו"ת הרשב"א ס' שצ"ה שכתב "עם כל זה מנעתי המנהג בעירנו" והבית יוסף השתמש בלשונו "שיש למנוע המנהג." ומה שכתב בראש הסימן "מנהג של שטות" הוא גם כן על יסוד לשון הרשב"א שם שכתב לענין אם השחיטה פסולה כמו שכתב ר"י בר מכיר

שיש חשש לפסול כמו השוחט לשם חטאתו, על זה השיב הרשב"א אי ני רואה לפסול השחיטה מפני שלא פסלו אלא השוחט לשם דבר הנידר והנידב, ודוקא תמימים אבל לא בעלי מומין, לפי כל הרואה יודע שאין זה לשם עולה ולשם שלמים דוקא, אלא "דברי הבאי בעלמא," ועל סמך לשונו כתב "מנהג של שטות," וכנראה שכך פירש בלשון הרשב"א גם בני"ד.

ובעיקר הדבר נראה לי היות שנתגלה לנו כמה תשובות הגאונים בענין זה וביחוד תשובת הגאונים אסף (חלק ב צד שה) וגנזי שכטר (חלק ב צד יח), שלדבריהם מפורש מנהג זה בגמ' כתובות ה לענין ערב יוהכ"פ גזירה שמא נשחט בן עוף עיי"ש בתו"י. והגאונים היתה להם קבלה שהסכימה למנהג זה אם כן מה שכתב הרשב"א "אף על פי," שלא היה לפניו דברי הגאונים, כמו שכתב שמעתי שנשאל רב האי גאון ואמר שכן נהגו ולפנינו, יש קרוב לעשרה מקורות, ראה בהערות אסף לתשובות הגאונים הנ"ל, ומ"ש בהערות לגנז"ש שם עמ' קכ"ג והגהות בשערי תשובה סי' רצט.

המדייק בתשובת הרשב"א רואה שהוא כתב מנעתי המנהג "בעירנו" הוסיף בציון גדול "בעירנו" מפני ששם הי' מנהג מוזר וז"ל, היה שוחטין תרנגולת זקן לכפרה לכל הנער היולד וחותכין ראשו ותולין הראש בנוצתו בפתח הבית עם שומים, והבלים הרבה שנראו בעיני כדרכי האמורי, ודחקתי על זה הדבר ובחסד עליון נשמעו דברי ולא נשאר מכל זה ומכיוצא באלו בעירנו מאומה ע"כ. ולפי זה מבואר להדיא שרק בעירו שהיה להם מנהגים מוזרים שיש בהם איסור גמור של דרכי האמורי, וכדי לעקר מלבם דבר זה מנע כל עיקר דבר זה של מנהג כפרות, אבל לא פסק לעקר מנהג זה בכל מקום. ודחה דברי ר"י בן מכיר שחשש לפסול השוחט בחוץ. נשאר רק המקור היחידי שכתב הארחות חיים דין עיוהכ"פ, והרמב"ן ז"ל אוסר מנהג זה משום דרכי האמורי, ואין לנו עוד מקור לזה וברור לי זה הי' המקורות הנ"ל לפני הבית יוסף לא היה כותב מה שכתב.

אמנם מצד אחר רואים שמרן הבית יוסף שכתב שיש למנוע מנהג זה לדורות, כיון ברוח קדשו לאמתה של תורה, כי הרבה גדולים בדורות האחרונים אמרו כן מטעם אחר שנולדו סבות אחרות שיש לבטל מנהג זה, היות שמרוב הכפרות נולדו ספקות בנוגע להשחיטה שיש בהם חשש נבלה, ראה במשנה ברורה וערוך השלחן ועוד. ולכן יש נוהגין לעשות כן במשך כל השבוע ויש

139 Hebrew Sources

שעושים כפרה בממון, או כמנהג שהביא רש"י שבת פא, וראה
ס' כתר שם טוב מנהג עיוהכ"פ.

לב.   חוט השני להרה"ג ר' נסים קארליץ שליט"א

מנהג הכפרות קשה לומר שיש נוהגין לעשותו דוקא על מעות
כיון דהמנהג לעשות על עופות הוא מנהג של כלל ישראל
ובאחרונים דחזינן שנשתמשו במעות לכפרה הוא רק כשאי
אפשר על כן מה שיש נמנעים לעשות על עופות קשה לומר
שהוא מנהג ולענין ההנהגה למעשה אפשר לעשות על עופות
ואפשר לעשות על מעות ומרן החזו"א נהג לעשות כפרות על
תרנגול.

GLOSSARY

Achan — the man who stole from the consecrated booty of Yericho. He was subjected to the death penalty for this violation.

Acharonim —lit., "later ones"; rabbis and *halachic* decisors from the 16th century to the present.

Akeidah— the binding of Yitzchak (Isaac). At G-d's behest, Avraham bound and prepared to offer his only son Yitzchak as a *korban*.

American bison (buffalo)—large shaggy-haired brown mammal of the North American plains.

anterior— of or near the head or toward the front of a body.

Arba Misos Beis Din—the four capital punishments, *sekilah, sereifah, hereg,* and *chenek* imposed by *Beis Din.*

Arizal—acronym for **A**doneinu **R**abbi **Y**itzchok **L**uria *zichrono l'verachah*—our master Rabbi Yitzchok of blessed memory—the most famous *mekubal* of all time.

Aseres Yemei Teshuvah—the first ten days of the year spanning from Rosh Hashanah through Yom Kippur. These days more than any are designated for doing *teshuvah.*

Ashkenaz—Germany.

asscera—a particularly painful childhood disease that causes swelling in the throat and eventual death through suffocation.

auspice—a sign of something to come, especially something important or bad.

aveiros—(Hebrew) sins.

Avodah—service of Hashem, preformed by the *Kohanim* in the Beis HaMikdash.

avodah zarah—the service of an entity other than G-d.

Avos—the Patriarchs.

Avraham Avinu—the first of the Patriarchs.

ba'al tashchis—the Biblical prohibition against needless waste.

beheimah (pl.—*beheimos*)—class of animals that includes cattle, sheep and goats, frequently translated as domesticated animals.

Beis Din—a religious court.

Beis HaMikdash—the Temple in Yerushalayim.

Beis Yosef – See Karo, Rabbi Yosef.

bentch gomel—to recite a special prayer of thanksgiving when rescued from serious harm.

berachah—a brief payer recited before performing a mitzvah (or consuming food).

berachah levatalah—a *berachah* said in vain.

kapitel (pl.—*kapitlach*)—(Yiddish from Latin) lit., capital; a Biblical chapter; a chapter of Psalms.

chayah (pl.—*chayos*)—a class of wild animals that require *kisuy hadam* when slaughtered.

Chayei Adam—the popular *halachic* work of Rabbi Avrohom Danzig (5508-5580; 1748–1820).

Chazal—a Hebrew acronym for **Chachamenu zichronom l'verachah**, our Sages of blessed memory.

chenek—strangulation, one of the punishments imposed by *Beis Din* for capital offenses.

Chosech—the name of the *malach* in charge of granting life.

Chullin—the 32nd tractate of the Gemara that covers many of the laws governing kosher meat.

chumrah—a voluntarily assumed restriction or stringency.

crop—a special pouch for the storage of food in the throat of most birds. Its presence is an indication of kosher status.

dam hanefesh—lit., soul blood; the blood needed for life.

darkei ha'emori—an *avodah zarah*-style custom.

Darkei Moshe—commentary on the *Tur* authored by the Rama.

divining—perceive through some inexplicable perceptive powers.

drumette—the section of a chicken's wing closest to the body that resembles a drumstick.

Erev Rosh Hashanah—the eve of Rosh Hashanah.

Erev Yom Kippur—the eve of Yom Kippur.

esophagus—the passage between the pharynx (mouth) and the stomach.

eviscerate—to remove the internal organs (innards) from the abdomen of an animal carcass.

fallow deer—a common species of deer native to western Eurasia. It has been introduced widely elsewhere, including many parts of the United States.

Feinstein, HaGaon Reb Dovid—successor to his father HaGaon Rav Moshe as Rosh Yeshiva of Mesivta Tiferes Jerusalem and Kollel Beth Medrash L'Torah V'Horaah, and leading *halachic* authority in the United States.

gemar tov—lit., a good ending; an expression meaning "good outcome" or "happy ending."

Gemara—the Talmud; the Oral Torah; the Code of Jewish Law.

Geonim – a group of Babylonian sages who lived just after the completion of the Talmud. They were the first to attempt to elucidate the Talmud.

gever— strength; man; rooster.

gevurah—strength; kabalistic term

gizzard—see *pupikal*.

Hakadosh Baruch Hu—The Holy One Blessed be He; a title for G-d.

halachah (pl.—*halachos*)—Jewish law(s).

half *shekel*—*machatzis hashekel*, the half shekel coin that every Jewish male was required to contribute annually for the Beis HaMikdash service.

hashkafah/hashkafic—[Jewish] moral perspective.

hataras nedarim—annulment of vows. A procedure in which the maker of an oath can appear before a court to seek annulment of his vows. When granting the request the court pronounces *mutar lach* (it is permitted to you), *mutar lach, mutar lach*, three times.

hereg—death by sword, one of the capital punishments imposed by *Beis Din*.

hilchos milichah—the laws governing the salting of kosher meat.

hock joint—a joint in the leg of a domestic fowl between the tibia (drumstick – *pulka*) and the shank (the yellow scaly lower part of a chicken's leg). It corresponds to the human ankle but bends in the opposite direction. The hock joint is sometimes mistakenly called the knee.

home-style *kashering*—the method used to *kasher* meat or poultry at home.

issur—a prohibition.

Iyov—one of the twenty-four books of *Tanach*; the name of the central figure in the book of the same name.

Kabbalah—lit., the Tradition; the study of Hashem.

Kaf Hachaim—the *halachic* work of Rav Yosef Chaim Sofer (born in Baghdad, 5630/1870, died in Yerushalyim, 5699/ 1939)

kaparos—the ceremony of revolving a chicken overhead and then *shechting* it in order to arouse the participant to *teshuvah*.

Karo, Rav Yosef—Rabbi Yosef (ben Ephraim) Karo (born in Toledo, Spain 5248/1488, died in Tzfas, Eretz Yisrael, 13 Nisan 5335/1575), co-author of the *Shulchan Aruch*. He codified Jewish law into the *Shulchan Aruch* in the 16th century. Also known as Mechaber—the Compiler—and Beis Yosef, the name of his other work.

kasher (kashered)—to render fit; the process of salting meat to purge it of blood and make it edible.

Kasher, Rabbi M. Mendel—(1895–1983) a Polish-born *rav* and prolific author most famous for his *magnum opus, Torah Sheleimah*—an encyclopedic work on the Torah.

Kiddush Hachodesh—the procedure for establishing the new month. When all the prerequisites have been resolved the head of the court rises and announces *"mekudash."* The other members of the court respond *"mekudash, mekudash,"* three times in total.

King Yoshiyahu—the 18th king of the Davidic dynasty, killed in battle with King Necho of Egypt.

kisuy hadam—the requirement to cover the blood of a bird or *chayah* with dirt after *shechitah*.

Kitzur Shulchan Aruch—a well-known, easy-to-read and authoritative compendium of common *halachos*.

Klal Yisrael—the Jewish Nation.

Kohen Gadol—the highest ranking priest, most important Beis HaMikdash functionary.

Kohen—a priest who served in the Beis HaMikdash.

korban chatas—a sin-offering *korban* brought as part of atoning for one of several major transgressions.

korban (pl.—*korbanos*)—one of various (often animal) offerings brought on the *mizbe'ach* in the Beis HaMikdash.

korban nedavah—voluntary gift offering brought on the *mizbe'ach* in the Beis HaMikdash.

Kosher Salt—coarse salt intended specifically for preparing meat for kosher consumption.

kosher—food fit for consumption; any item fit for its intended purpose.

laws of *milichah*—see HILCHOS MILICHAH.

Levush—the halachic work of Rav Mordecai ben Avraham Yoffe (born in Prague c. 1530, died in Posen March 7, 1612)

m'derabonan—of rabbinical origin.

Machzor Vitri—the *halachic* work of Rav Simchah ben Shmuel of Vitri (died 1105), a French Talmudist of the 11th and 12th centuries and pupil of Rashi.

machzor (pl.—*machzorim*)—lit. cycle; a book of halachah and *tefillos* for the yearly cycle.

Maharal—Rav Yehuda Loeb ben Bezalel (c. 1520–17 September 1609), widely known as the Maharal of Prague. MaHaRaL is the Hebrew acronym of **Mo**reinu **HaRav** Loeb. He served as the leading rabbi in the city of Prague in Bohemia for most of his life.

Mahari Veil—**Mo**reinu **HaR**av **Y**acov ben Yehudah Veil (died 1456). A *talmid* of the Maharil and often quoted by the Rama, he is most famous for his *teshuvos*.

Maharil—Moreinu HaRav Yacov ben Moshe Halevi Moelin (c. 1365–1427). He was a Talmudist and *posek* best known for his codification of the *minhagim* of the *Ashkenazi* Jews. Maharil's *minhagim* was a primary source for the Rama's component of the *Shulchan Aruch*.

malach—an angel.

malkos— the thirty-nine lashes *Beis Din* administers for minor infractions.

maaser funds—one-tenth of one's earnings, often designated as funds for charity or other *mitzvos*. According to many authorities this tithe is mandatory and the funds are not considered one's own. They may not be used towards fulfilling one's monetary obligations.

m'deoraysa—according to Torah Law.

Mechaber—See Karo, Rabbi Yosef.

mefarshim—commentators.

Meiri—Rabbi Menachem ben Solomon Meiri (1249–1316) was a Provincial scholar and commentator of the Talmud. His commentary, the *Beis Habechirah*, is a monumental work on the entire Talmud.

mekil—lenient.

mesorah—the tradition handed down through the generations, often concerning a particular interest (i.e., the identification of kosher birds) or the manner how something is to be done.

metzorah—someone suffering from an illness similar to leprosy. The *metzorah* is *tamei* and must endure a lengthy and involved process to become *tahor*.

Mikro'os Gedolos—lit., a large format *Chumash*, often used as a title for a *Chumash* printed with the standard commentaries.

milichah—lit., salting; salting meat to draw out the blood, part of the *kashering* process.

minhag—a custom.

Mishnah Berurah—a work of halachah by Rabbi Yisrael Meir Kagan, the Chofetz Chaim (5588–5693/1838–1933).

misos—lit., death; term for capital punishments imposed by *Beis Din*.

mitzvah (pl.—*mitzvos*)—a Torah commandment.

mizbe'ach—an altar; the structure in the courtyard of the Beis HaMikdash upon which the sacrifices were burnt.

necromancy—the belief in magical spells that harness occult forces or evil spirits to produce unnatural effects in the world.

neveilah (pl.—*neveilos*)—carrion, an animal that died without proper *shechitah*.

olay regel—pilgrims, people who visit the Beis HaMikdash on the three major festivals (*Regalim*).

omen—a sign of something to come, especially something important or bad.

open—short for "open back *kashering*." It is industry jargon for a chicken that has been split along the spine, from the neck area on top until the tail area on bottom, to facilitate efficient *kashering*.

pasken—to render a *halachic* decision.

pasuk (pl.—*pesukim*)—a biblical verse.

pasul—cause(d) to be *halachically* invalid.

Pirkei D'Rebbe Eliezer—a *medrash* attributed to the *Tana*, Rebbe Eliezer Hagadol.

Pesach—the first of the three major festivals (*Regalim*).

Peskita—a *medrash* on the *Haftoras* attributed to the *Amora* Rebbe Kahanah.

pesukim—see PASUK.

Pnei Yehoshua—Rabbi Yaakov Yehoshua ben Tzvi Hirsch Falk (Cracow–Offenbach am Main, 1680–1756). He was a Polish and German rabbi and Talmudist. On his mother's side he was a grandson of Rabbi Yehoshua Heschel of Cracow, author of *Magine Shelomoh*.

posek (pl.—*poskim*)—*halachic* decisor(s).

Pri Megadim—a *halachic* work by Rav Yosef ben Meir Teomim (1727–1792). He was a Galician rabbi who wrote *sefarim* on all topics in Judaism. His most famous work, *Pri Megadim* on *Shulchan Aruch*, is a super commentary on the *Taz*, *Shach* and *Magen Avraham*.

psak—*halachic* decision.

pulka—a leg (of a chicken); a drumstick.

pupik/pupikal—the gizzard, an organ in the chicken's digestive tract that grinds the food, comparable to the stomach of a mammal.

quail—(*coturnix coturnix*) a small, kosher, migrating bird native to Eurasia.

Radvaz—**R**abbi **D**avid **b**en Shlomo ibn (**A**bi) **Z**imra. A contemporary of Rav Yosef Karo, he was a leading *posek*, Rosh Yeshiva, chief rabbi and author of more than 3,000 responsa, as well as several scholarly works. Born in Spain around 1479, he was thirteen years of age when he was banished from Spain. He first settled in Safed and then moved to Fes and later Cairo.

ram of Yitzchak—the ram that was offered as a *korban* in place of Yitzchak Avinu. See *Akeidah*.

Rama—acronym for **R**abbi **M**oshe **I**sserles, born and died in Cracow, Poland, (c. 5280–18 Iyar (Lag Ba'omer) 5332/c. 1520– May 1, 1572); co-author of *Shulchan Aruch*.

Ramban—**R**abbi **M**oshe **b**en **N**achman, also known as Nachmanides (4954–c. 5029/1194–c. 1270). He was born in Porta, Barcelona, studied in Girona (hence his name "Girondi") and died in Eretz Yisrael. He wrote many famous works on the Talmud and halachah.

Rami bar Tamri—a Talmudic sage.

Rashba—**R**abbi **Sh**lomo **b**en **A**deres (1235–1310) was born in Barcelona, Spain. He wrote many famous works on the Talmud and halachah.

Rashi—**R**abbi **S**hlomo [ben] **Y**itzchaki was born in Troyes, Champagne, in northern France (4800–4865/1040–1105). He wrote the most famous and widely used commentary on *Tanach* and the Talmud.

rav (pl.—*Rabbanim*)—a rabbi (who is a *halachic* decisor).

Rav Hai Gaon—Rav Hai (ben Sherira) Gaon (939–1038) was a medieval rabbi and scholar who served as *Gaon* of Pumbeditha during the early 11th century. He received his education from his father, Rav Sherira (Gaon) ben Chanina. He was the last and probably most famous *Gaon*.

Rebbe Chanina ben Dosa—a well-known Mishnaic sage known in particular for his ability to pray.

Rishonim—lit., "early ones"; the rabbinic scholars between the 11th and 16th centuries.

Rosh Hashanah—the holiday observed on the first day of the year; the day the world is judged.

Rosh—**R**abbenu **Osh**er (ben Yechiel) was born in western Germany and died in Toledo, Spain (5010 or 5019–9 Cheshvan 5089/1250 or 1259–1328). He wrote many famous works on the Talmud and halachah.

rov—majority (of a *shiur*)

sa'ir hameshtale'ach—the young he-goat cast down a cliff (outside of Yerushalayim) as part of the Temple service on Yom Kippur.

Satan—evil inclination, prosecutor.

Sefardim—Jews whose ancestors originated from Spain. They generally follow the *halachic* opinions of the Mechaber.

sefer (pl.—*sefarim*)—book(s), especially works on holy subjects.

Sefer HaOrah—a compilation of Rashi's *halachic* rulings prepared by his student, Rabbi Nathan Hamachiri.

sekilah—stoning, one of the punishments imposed by *Beis Din* for capitol offenses.

semichah—lit., leaning; placing of hands on the head of a *korban* to recite the *Viduy*.

semichas zekainim—a process in which the Elders place their hands on the head of a student to pass the mantle of leadership to the student.

sereifah—burning, one of the punishments imposed by *Beis Din* for capitol offenses.

Shacharis—morning prayers.

shaliach Beis Din—a court officer/clerk.

shaliach tzibbur—the communal representative, often leads the *tefillos* in shul.

Shavous—the second of the three major festivals (*Regalim*).

shechitah (shechting) — the act of slaughtering an animal according to Torah law.

Shehechiyanu — a special blessing said on seasonal *mitzvos* or joyous occasions, among other times.

shechutei chutz — the offense of offering a *korban* outside of the Beis HaMikdash.

shemitah — the final year of the seven year cycle during which the fields must be left fallow.

Shibbolei HaLeket — Tzedekiah ben Avrohom HaRofe of the Anavim family (1210–1275). He lived in Rome and received his Talmudic training in Rome and in Germany.

shlita — a Hebrew acronym for "*Sheyichye l'orech yamim tovim aruchim* — May he live many long and good days." A blessing offered to a prestigious person.

shlug kaparos — (Yiddish) to swing *kaparos*.

shochet — a ritual slaughterer.

Shulchan Aruch — the primary compendium of halachah (Torah Law), co-authored by Rabbi Yosef Karo and Rabbi Moshe Isserles.

sifter cap — a cap with medium-sized holes, often fitted on spice containers.

siman (pl. — *simanim*) — the foods eaten on the eve of Rosh Hashanah, meant to serve as a good omen; chapters of *Shulchan Aruch*.

Succos — the third of the three major festivals (*Regalim*). On the final day of this Yom Tov a special ceremony was held in the Beis HaMikdash, during which the *kohanim* circled the *mizbe'ach* seven times.

swallowing tract — the tubes and organs in the throat that carry the food down to the stomach/gizzard.

tachti—in my stead.

talmid—a student.

Talmud—the authoritative collection of ancient rabbinic writings of Jewish law and tradition, the Oral Law.

Tanach—an acronym for *Torah, Nevi'im,* and *Kesuvim,* the twenty-four books of the Written Torah.

Tehillim—one of the twenty-four books of *Tanach,* the Book of Psalms.

temurah—exchange, an illegal exchange of sanctity from a *korban* animal to a non-*korban* animal.

teshuvah (pl.—*teshuvos*)—repentance, a multi step process of returning to Hashem; a *halachic* responsa.

Teshuvos Hageonim—a collection of responsa of close to ninety rabbis who lived and worked in the centuries following the completion of the Talmud. The work is principally responsa on Talmudical interpretation and *halachic* practice. The period of the *Geonim* stretched from approximately 4350 (589) and lasted until about 4800 (1040). The majority of the *teshuvos* were published over the course of the 19th century.

thaumaturgy—an art that invokes supernatural powers, magical feats.

Tishrei—the seventh month of the year. Rosh Hashanah, Yom Kippur and Succos all fall in the month of Tishrei.

Tosfos—lit., addendum (to *Rashi*); glosses printed on the margin of the Talmud authored by a group of medieval scholars.

treif—lit., torn; non-kosher.

tevilah—immersion in a *mikvah*.

Tur— Rabeinu Yacov ben Osher, (Cologne, Germany c.1269 and likely died in Toledo, Spain c.1343). He was an influential *halachic* authority. He is often referred to as the Baal Haturim (or Tur for short), after his main *halachic* work, the *Arba Turim*. He was the third son of Rabbi Osher ben Yechiel (known as the Rosh).

tzaddik—a righteous person.

tza'ar ba'alei chaim—the Biblical prohibition against causing needless pain to an animal.

tzedakah—lit., ethical; right or proper; charity.

tziduk hadin—acceptance of judgment; a prayer said at a funeral.

veich-schissel—lit., a softening basin; a basin used to soak meat and poultry in preparation for the *kashering* process.

veshet—see esophagus.

viduy—the avowal of one's sin before G-d; confession said when bringing a *korban*, on Yom Kippur or before death.

viscera—internal organs collectively, especially those in the abdominal cavity.

wrangler—one who tends or cares for animals.

Yehoshua (bin Nun)—Moshe's successor as the second leader of the Jewish People. He led the successful campaign to conquer Eretz Yisrael for the *Yidden*. His first conquest was the city of Yericho.

Yericho—a city in Eretz Yisrael; the first city conquered by Yehoshua during the conquest of Eretz Yisrael.

Yidden—(Yiddish) Jews.

Yiddishkeit –Judaism.

Yom Kippur—Day of Atonement, the tenth day of Tishrei.

zalts-brettal—lit., salting-board; a perforated board that allows the blood-tainted secretions to drain during the *kashering* process.

zt"l—a Hebrew acronym for "*Zecher tzaddik l'verachah*—May the memory of the righteous be blessed."

zeh chalifasi—this is my exchange. A phrase recited during the *kaparos* ceremony.

zera—seed; offspring.

zocheh—worthy, meritorious.

INDEX

Step-By-Step Pictorial Guide to Kashering

The cleaned chicken lying on a cardboard sheet on my outdoor table. Working outdoors allows me to keep the mess (and cleaning chickens can be messy!) outside.

Preparing to remove the feet and wings. Bend the foot at the joint. Plan to cut exactly in the middle of the yellow knob.

Use a good quality poultry scissors (available in all houseware stores) or a sharp knife to slice through the joint. Notice that the cut is in the middle of the joint, not above or below it.

Almost through. Then repeat for the second leg.

Next, remove the wing tips. Lift and extend the wing. In the chicken pictured, the flying feathers were cleaned from the wingette. However, those feathers are the hardest to clear and the novice is advised not to bother with them. Instead, the beginner should cut the wing at the lower joint and remove the wingette.

Again, aim to cut in the middle of the joint. Repeat for the second wing. Then remove the head.

Head, wings and feet are all neatly trimmed off.

The exposed neck. The white streak in the center (partly colored red) is the vein that must be removed. The other white streaks, above and below, are the neck ligaments.

Pull the vein gently but firmly to remove it. (If it rips, it is treated as cut, which is also acceptable, see Chapter 12, "Whole Chickens #12".)

A quail with the vein clearly visible

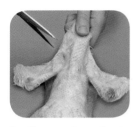

Another option is to remove the neck altogether. Aim to cut as close to the base as possible.

Cutting away the loosened skin makes kashering easier.

You are now ready to open the chicken and remove the gut. Locate the tip of the breast and cut right below it. Be gentle and go slow. If you cut deeply you may sever the guts.

Easy does it. Make small cuts.

Start with a small hole like this.

Widen it slowly.

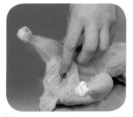

This is about as wide a hole you want to cut.

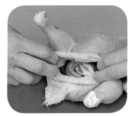

Now pull it the rest of the way apart by hand.

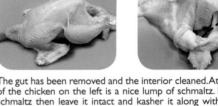

The gut has been removed and the interior cleaned. At the front of the chicken on the left is a nice lump of schmaltz. If you like schmaltz then leave it intact and kasher it along with the rest of the chicken. If you don't appreciate schmaltz then remove and discard it now. Notice how the extended left leg creates a hollow. You must salt all sides of the interior of this pocket. An easy way to access this area (and eliminate the pocket) is by making a small slit in the skin as indicated in the picture.

Start from the neck area and cut along the spine.

The coagulated blood visible beneath the skin (on the bends of the wings) in this and several other pictures will dissolve and disappear when the chicken is soaked.

Cut straight down the back.

Remove tail (oil glands).

Cut along the other side of the spine. Remove spine and discard.

Spine and tail removed.

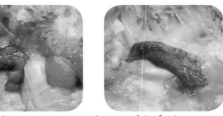

The opened chicken. Bits of lungs and the kidneys are visible (the last two pictures are closeups of the first). This is how a "kashered open" chicken looks (albeit a little cleaner) before salting.

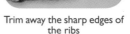

To continue cutting the chicken into quarters, lift it by the leg and cut between the "top" and "bottom."

Trim away the sharp edges of the ribs

The prepared breasts

The three usable pieces of chicken; the top (in one piece) and the bottoms (quartered)

Foil pan recast as zalts-brettal

The birds soaking in a lined pail of water. Notice how the top of the neck extends above the water. This is a problem and should be rectified.

The cleaned and soaked bird. You are now ready to start salting. It is wise to begin salting inside the cavity.

It is always easiest to salt the inside first. Aim your salt into the cavity from the openings on top and bottom.

Zeh Kaporosi

Make sure to get all sides of every piece. Lift win

Loose skin can be a challenge. You must lift the edge in order to get the salt beneath it.

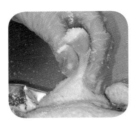

Don't forget to do the tips.

Salt the remainder of the bird.

Position the bird in a way that none of the excretions can collect in the cavity or on the surface around the bird. In this picture the back of the duck is raised so that all the fluids from inside drain nicely through the hole at the top, near the neck.

Safely away from the excreted brine. The disposable plate in this picture is catching the brine. This brine is treif. Were it to drip on the counter or other utensil, those items would become treif.

A pile of salted quails. The meat may be stacked as the salt does its job. Notice that they are arranged in a manner that prevents liquid from gathering inside or between them. and positioned safely away from the accumulating brine.

The pupik (gizzard) with the proventriculus still attached

Use a sharp knife and cut around the outer side. Stop just before the inner sac.

The muscle has been cut through and the inner sac is still intact. With a firm motion pull the remainder of the muscle apart.

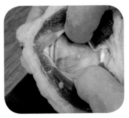

Slowly peel the edible meat off the inner sac.

If you cut into the sac, you should still try to remove it in one piece. If that is not possible, open the sac fully and wash the whole gizzard well. Once it is cleaned, carefully peel the inner membrane from the meat.

TEKUFAS HASHANAH SERIES

The *Tekufas Hashanah* series provides a refreshing, hands-on approach to certain *mitzvos* that have not been easily accessible to the layman. The books are distinguished by the clarity of their language, their down-to-earth style, the beauty of their photography, their eye-catching layout, and most of all their purpose: the demystification of *mitzvos* that people might otherwise be hesitant to approach. The reader, led along by a master teacher, emerges from the experience well-informed and empowered.

Teka Beshofar

Teka Beshofar is a clear, user-friendly, highly effective guide to *shofar*-blowing. It is the first work of its kind and is appealing to all ages and levels. Even small children will be drawn in by the captivating photographs of various *shofaros* and of the animals that grow these marvelous horns. Written in a folksy style, this book is the perfect companion for a person who is embarking upon the exciting adventure of *tekias shofar*. Its step-by-step approach works as well for someone who is scared to put a *shofar* to his lips as it does for an experienced blower who is looking to perfect his skills. The book is filled with practical tips and sound advice that can not only jumpstart a beginner, but also help a seasoned *ba'al tekiah* improve his performance.

Read it and you will see that shofar-blowing is much easier than you imagined.

Lekicha Tama

Oh no—it's that time of year again! The hustle and bustle, the scrutinizing and haggling… it's time to buy your *lulav* and *esrog*. You thought you learned the pertinent *halachos*, but the shopping experience is still totally overwhelming. Is the *esrog* you're holding a *mehudar*? Your *lulav* isn't perfect, but is it *kosher*? At what point do your drooping, darkened *aravos* become *posul*? The answers to these and other questions are now at the tips of your fingers. *Lekicha Tama*: The *Lulav* and *Esrog* Buying Guide, holds your hand as you pass through the marketplace confronting these and other questions. With a wealth of information presented in an engaging style and clear photographs to illustrate its points, this *sefer* can provide even anadvanced student with insights into the pertinent *halachos*.

Chalutz Hana 'al

Chalitza is an enigma to most people. Even those who have learned *Maseches Yevamos* and have some inkling about the ceremony have never actually viewed one. No more need to imagine! Here, for the first time in English, is a clear description — along with thirty-three color photos — of a *chalitza*. This one-of-a-kind *sefer* opens a previously shuttered window into the *mitzvah*, which until now has been the exclusive domain of a handful of scholars. What is the sequence of events at a *chalitza*? What do participants say and do in the course of the ceremony? What does the special shoe look like? What is the purpose of this mitzvah and of the various steps involved in its performance? Read *Chalutz Hana'al* and find out.